ROOM
for
CHANGE

ROOM *for*
CHANGE

Linda Gray

THAMES MACDONALD

A THAMES MACDONALD BOOK
© Thames Macdonald 1988

First published in Great Britain in 1988
by Macdonald & Co (Publishers) Ltd
London & Sydney
a member of Maxwell Pergamon
Publishing Corporation plc

*British Library Cataloguing in
Publication Data*
Gray, Linda, 1948–
    Room for change.
    1. Interior decoration
    I. Title
    747   NK2110

ISBN 0–356–15521–8

Filmset by MS Filmsetting Limited,
Frome, Somerset
Printed and bound in Great Britain by
Purnell Book Production, Paulton,
near Bristol

Senior Commissioning Editor:
Joanna Lorenz
Art Director: Linda Cole
Text Editor: John Wainwright
Designer: Michael Wade with
Muffy Dodson
Room Set Photographer:
Graham Henderson
Stylist: Dee Martyn
Step-by-step Illustrations: Coral Mula

Macdonald & Co (Publishers) Ltd
Greater London House
Hampstead Road
London NW1 7QX

Contents

Introduction

Who creates the rooms featured in magazines and interior design books – and who lives in them? The designers are often anonymous figures and the owners may be conspicuous by their absence, making it difficult for the reader to judge whether the decor is right for their own lifestyles. So welcome to Room For Change, where every picture is based on a real room, and a real-life family and their problems.

In the following pages we introduce you to a young couple in their first flat, a businessman and his family who live over the shop, two professionals in their thirties with growing daughters, a design-conscious couple with a small son and a large dog, a two-year-old toddler (and his parents), and a pair of newlyweds. Each had a problem room which needed the attention of experts in design and decorating, and Room For Change was delighted to help.

To give the owners a choice of scheme, Room For Change asked three designers to look at each room. As you will discover from the short biographies we have included, the eighteen decorators were not drawn exclusively from the world of interior design because professionals in related activities such as architecture, sculpture, textile design, the theatre and fine art also have a wealth of ideas to offer. Thus the living room was assigned to doyen of designers David Hicks, magazine stylist Susy Smith and interior design student Colin Fredricson. Architect Pedro Guedes, restaurateur Roy Ackerman and avant-garde architect Lynn Davis took on the kitchen while sculptor and furniture designer Cebuan de la Rochette, interior designer Colin Gold and theatrical designer Mick Hurd tackled the dining room. Society decorator Nicholas Haslam, curator and art historian Stephen Calloway and textile designer Cressida Bell sorted out the adult bedroom and the child's room was allocated to textile designer Jon Lys Turner, decorative painter Annie Sloan and children's TV presenter Floella Benjamin. Finally, artist Althea Wilson, design consultant Mary Fox Linton and architect Doug Patterson turned their attention to the bathroom.

As it was impractical to decorate each room three times *in situ*, Room For Change built a facsimile of each in the studio and invited the owners along to compare the results and declare a preference – and their opinions were as fascinating as the designer's interpretation of their needs and lifestyles.

You may recognize the characters in this drama from the Thames Television programme Room For Change. We thought you'd like a chance to study the rooms at leisure, and in addition to the finished designs we have included information on the original rooms and their owners, biographies of the designers, plans, swatches and, of course, DIY instructions to help you achieve that designer look in your own home. Is there Room For Change at your house? Read on to find out.

Linda Gray

The living room is the public face of the home, which is why it takes top priority in most furnishing budgets. Though the best parties may end in the kitchen, they begin in the living room so the decor has to be stimulating, attractive and hard wearing. Quite apart from parties, the living room has to cater for a number of unrelated and even contradictory activities. In most homes this is where children play, adults relax and families listen to music, watch TV and eat together – often all at the same time!

Designing and decorating such a multi-functional room, often in a space which measures less than 6 by 4 metres (20 by 12ft) requires careful consideration. For example, obviously seating is required, but why automatically opt for a traditional three-piece suite? Two sofas might prove a better bet. They allow various options as far as the layout of the room is concerned: identical sofas can be placed opposite each other, with a coffee table in between; or two and three seaters pushed together in a L shape. Moreover, some antique and modern styles can sit harmoniously together in the same room, and individual chairs can be added to accommodate different seating preferences – chaise longues for those who want to stretch out, and upright, high-back chairs for those who like to keep their feet firmly on the ground.

Storage and display space is almost as important as seating. Space must be allocated to absorb the high-tech clutter of videos, compact discs and stereos; china and books, which are used as well as displayed, and purely ornamental items, such as photographs. Surfaces will be needed for the constant flow of coffee cups, magazines, letters and snacks which drift across the typical living room; hence the need for occasional tables. And some homes may require space to be set aside for a dining table, attractive enough for a dinner party and yet not too smart for homework or children's games.

Finally, the entire setting should be carefully lit and stylishly presented to create a real room for living. All in all, a task which can daunt the average DIY decorator – which is why you should look at how our three designers tackled the problem.

The Living Room

THE ORIGINAL LIVING ROOM

Paul Yeadon, a qualified surveyor, and Inger Cessford, a senior account manager in a sales promotions agency, are a young couple living in a converted ground floor flat in South London. As they prefer to spend more of their income on sailing and entertaining than on home furnishings, they are keen to receive some ideas on low-budget, high-style redecoration.

First time buyers Paul Yeadon and Inger Cessford have been lucky in London's housing stakes, for their home is a spacious three bedroom flat which once formed the ground floor of a terraced house. It has been extended to provide accommodation that is more than adequate for their needs. In addition to the three bedrooms, there's a garden, a good kitchen and a large living room.

However, it was partly the size of the living room that concerned the couple. They felt it was cold and featureless, and although facing south-west and dominated by a deep Victorian bay window, it suffered from limited light. Even white painted walls had not helped dispel the gloom.

Most of the decor was very plain. The room was furnished with brown carpet and simple, modern upholstery; and bereft of period detail, such as the original fireplace and decorative mouldings. Paul and Inger were not bothered by this omission, being unimpressed by the vogue for Victorian revival – though Inger expressed an interest in using more decorative forms of wallcovering, such as borders, patterned wallpaper, or possibly a decorative paint treatment like sponging. 'I always tend to go for very neutral plain colours', she confessed, 'and I thought it was time to get away from that'.

Because Inger and Paul both have demanding careers, they agreed it was very important that their 'new' living room should be a place where they could relax and unwind. As entertainment, buying clothes and hobbies such as sailing dispose of much of their income, keeping to a reasonable budget was important, but, as they have no plans for children, the new decor wouldn't need to reflect the various constraints imposed by family life.

Their individual priorities differed: Inger was eager to use pale colours, such as lemon, to magnify the light; while Paul was more concerned with minimizing noise. One problem with the flat was inferior soundproofing – voices and footsteps resounded overhead, whilst a cellar below amplified sound within the room. Consequently, though Inger favoured the look of sealed floorboards, Paul expressed reservations because of the echoes and draughts he felt would inevitably ensue.

Both of them were happy to jettison their existing furnishings, with the exception of two antique pieces which had been in Paul's family for some time. The first was his grandfather's sea chest, which had circumnavigated Cape Horn

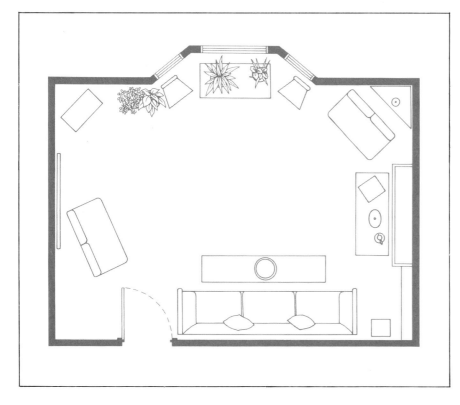

THERE'S ROOM FOR IMPROVEMENT IN THIS SPARSELY FURNISHED LIVING ROOM WHERE THE BULK OF THE FURNITURE IS CONCENTRATED IN ONE CORNER. THE FINE BAY WINDOW IS A NEGLECTED FEATURE AND THE WALL OPPOSITE THE CHIMNEY BREAST IS ALMOST COMPLETELY BLANK.

on countless occasions before coming to rest in Tooting. Now it supported a gramophone of equal vintage, as well as a modern music centre which Paul and Inger were anxious to conceal. The second item was a plain oak corner cabinet, originally used by Paul's grandmother to store glass.

Paul and Inger felt these pieces would add visual as well as sentimental warmth to the new room. 'I like the idea of having natural wood in the room', says Inger. 'I don't want it to look too stark and harsh,' Paul added, 'I

like older objects and I like older wood'. But how could the pieces best be accommodated in a late twentieth-century setting?

DESPITE ITS WHITE WALLS AND LARGE BAY WINDOW THE ORIGINAL LIVING ROOM LOOKS DULL AND DINGY. THE SCHEME IS BASED ON A SINGLE COLOUR — BROWN — AND IS DEVOID OF PATTERN. THE LACK OF PERIOD DETAIL SUCH AS A CORNICE OR A CHIMNEYPIECE ACCENTUATES THE DIVISION BETWEEN THE BARE WALLS AND THE FLOOR.

The Designer

I   David Hicks

Doyen of interior designers, David
Hicks began his career almost a
quarter of a century ago, when his use
of geometric design and brilliant
colour infused new energy into post-
war interior design. Revolutionary as
these ideas seemed at the time, his
passion for classical styles ensured that
the abstract motifs and vivid scarlet,
yellow and black colours (typical of
Hicks) were readily accepted by the
country house set, who form an
important part of his clientele.

Described as 'inordinately well
connected' (he is related to the Royal
Family via his wife, the former Lady
Pamela Mountbatten), David Hicks has
created interiors for the Prince of
Wales, the Princess Royal and sufficient
aristocrats to fill a substantial section
of Debrett's.

However, the Hicks touch is not
confined to British society, for his flair
and commercial acumen have enabled
him to extend his practice to private
and public clients in Europe, America
and the Middle East. Palaces,
department stores, hotels, ocean liners
and luxury yachts all bear the David
Hicks imprint – which is also available
to less exalted clients in the form of
furniture, textiles and carpets, from
his shop in Piccadilly.

David's attitude to the roller
coaster of design trends, which sees
the periodic revival of such contrasting
styles as the traditional country house
look, neo-classicism, Memphis chic and
high-tech, is that whilst taste is an
imprecise quality, and fashions will
always change, there are 'certain
elements of design which constitute
acceptable, interesting taste'. These
include a love of symmetry, an

appreciation of eighteenth- and
nineteenth-century forms and a liking
for strong colours as well as
pastels – although the latter are used in
Hicks' designs, they are perhaps not
immediately associated with his style.
Nor indeed are modest living rooms in
converted flats owned by couples
decorating on a tight budget. Which is

why Paul and Inger's room was as
challenging in its own way as a
commission to decorate a royal suite at
Windsor Castle or on the QE2.

Acid yellow, charcoal and black make a smart setting for Paul and Inger's antique sea chest and corner cabinet. Bookshelves and a dining table and chairs turn this into a multi-purpose room.

David Hicks' Design

The two most striking features of the living room David Hicks has designed for Paul and Inger are the acid yellow walls (a characteristic Hicks colour) and the formal arrangement of the furniture.

Everything that Paul and Inger

requested has been meticulously included in the layout. The utilitarian dining table, now concealed beneath a floor length cloth, is positioned in the bay window to form a square with the four upright chairs, the charcoal coloured sofa and the old sea chest.

David chose this symmetrical arrangement to reflect the shape of the

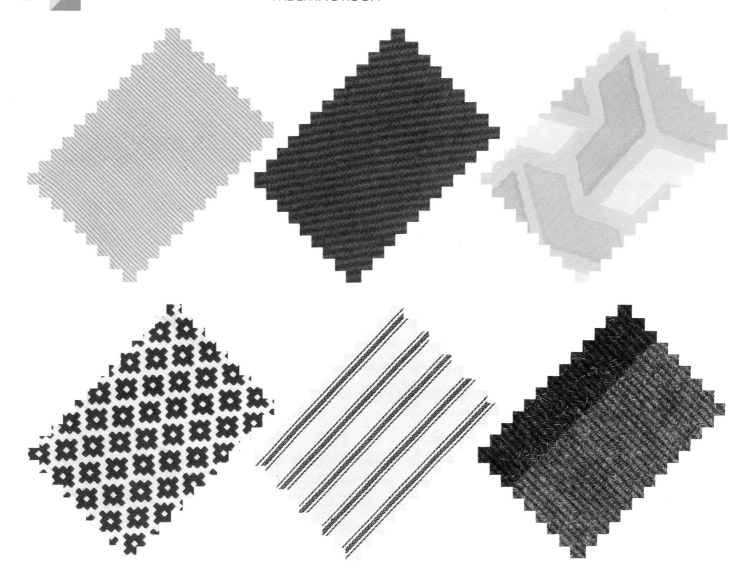

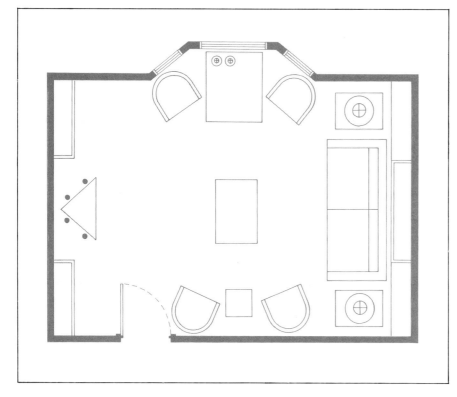

Above. David used his own distinctive designs for the curtains and tablecloth, with plain ticking for the dining chairs for economy. Bright pink cushions enliven the dark sofa, which is covered in charcoal to blend with the cord carpet.

The formal arrangement of furniture is more flexible than it may appear. The dining table and chairs can be moved to the centre of the room when required and a pair of upright chairs can be placed opposite the sofa to create a conversation group when Paul and Inger entertain.

Symmetry is an important element of David Hicks' schemes as his placing of the accessories and the furniture plan show.

room with its large, angled bay. However, he is keen to emphasise the adaptability of the layout; the chairs can be brought up to the table for dinner parties, or spread out to the corners of the room for a more casual, everyday look; whilst the sea chest, topped by a cushion, can provide extra seating, or be drawn up to the sofa to serve as a coffee table.

This arrangement ensures a clear view of the oak corner cupboard, now hoisted high on wooden struts. 'Originally it would have been made for a farmhouse or country cottage', says David – a far cry from SW17. 'However, it is quite valuable and they both like it, so I decided to make it the room's focal point.'

Beneath it nestles Paul and Inger's television. David is aware of the realities of life: 'on a sunny day the bay window will be the room's most important point', he says, 'but when it's not sunny the television will be more important'. Its position gives the viewer the effect of 'sitting in the dress circle at the cinema' – bringing a sense of occasion even to Eastenders. The set could however go inside the raised corner cupboard, minimising its impact on the room.

It's the West End, however, that's reflected in the sophisticated colour scheme. David chose yellow for the walls, 'because I thought it was particularly nice for this room, facing south as it does'; especially as, despite

its aspect, the room lacks light. Bright yellow gives the room character as well as warmth, and is offset by charcoal, which together 'add up to an interesting colour story'.

Though the major surfaces such as the walls, sofa and carpet are plain, pattern is introduced in the black and white striped ticking of the upright chairs and the diamond motif of the four curtains which define the bay. 'I do like geometrics', says David. 'I think they add character.' The character of this room is predominantly masculine, though a softer dimension is introduced by the pink cushions on the sofa and the tablecloth, which mingles pink and duck egg blue with yellow.

As much storage space as possible is packed into the room. Cupboards and shelves, painted yellow to blend in with the walls, are built out each side of the oak corner cupboard and set into the alcoves beside the chimney breast. David chose not to re-open the fireplace because 'it's not sensible in a smallish room' where every inch of wall space counts, and is unnecessary when a room is centrally heated.

The Hicks touch is further evident in accessories such as the black side tables, basalt vases and elegant table lamps (in pairs of course), which give the room an air of grandeur despite its limited size, However, most of the furnishings are not expensive: the carpet is grey cord; the walls are decorated with plain emulsion and dark grey ribbon and the chairs are upholstered in ticking, at £5 a metre. All in all, a scheme that's both stylish and budget conscious. 'It's not what it costs but what it looks like that counts', says David.

David Hicks' novel display unit for the corner cabinet consists of uprights which suspend it in mid air in the centre of the wall opposite the chimney breast. The black uprights mirror the charcoal ribbon border and ticking stripes.

Four curtains with an elegant pinch pleat heading emphasise the shape of the attractive bay window. Slim Venetian blinds screen the light and the view, and the floor area is filled by a compact dining table.

How to Put Up a Ribbon Border

As the scheme David Hicks designed for Paul and Inger shows, decorative borders not only add interest to otherwise plain walls, but also are a substitute for a missing cornice or picture rail. Moreover, they can be used to visually lower the height of high ceilings and they can, as in David's design, emphasise the symmetry of a room.

David chose a Petersham ribbon with an attractive ribbed texture, in charcoal grey – one of the dominant colours of his scheme. You might wish to choose a border with a stencilled floral or geometric motif, for example. But whatever you opt for, try to pick up colour and/or pattern from elsewhere in the room (such as the curtains or upholstery) to achieve a co-ordinated look. Remember, it is quite easy to copy a motif, cut out your own stencil (see page 34) and transfer it to ribbon (or paper).

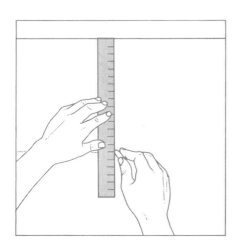

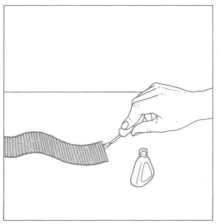

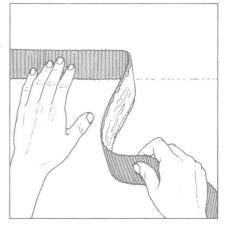

1 Measure down from ceiling in several places, to depth required. Join up marks with chalk to form continuous line around walls. Because of irregularities between ceiling and walls, check line *looks* straight, and adjust so it meets in line at corners.

2 Cut ribbon to length and, if you are designing your own, stencil motif(s) onto it using fabric paint (see page 34). It is a good idea to coat the cut ends with clear nail varnish to prevent fraying.

3 Spread a latex adhesive (such as Copydex) onto back, paying particular attention to edges and ends. Stick ribbon into position, following and covering the chalk line. Butt joint ends of lengths together, taking care not to stretch the ribbon.

The Designer

2 Colin Fredricson

Resplendent in black leather bedecked with studs, spurs and a silver bat; his hair augmented by a black pony tail, and his face made up with a black beauty spot and eyeliner, Fred is a walking affirmation of the Gothic style he embraces.

Fred, aka Colin Fredricson, HND student of interior design at the London College of Furniture, is no purist – his clothing owes more to punk than the Pre-Raphaelites. But his work is, he claims, profoundly influenced by ideas which were current in the fourteenth century and later romanticised in the nineteenth.

Fred's own room in a council flat in a run-down East End block reveals his style at its most extravagant. A broken mirror is surmounted by a crucifix, red crescents are daubed on the walls and corrugated iron is draped with swags of black net; even the bedding is spattered with black. A series of Gothic shrines, including one to that contemporary icon Marilyn Monroe, and a montage of photos and paintings by Fred himself, all illuminated by the candles and oil lamps he prefers to twentieth century tungsten light, complete the picture.

Already, Fred has created interiors for a jeweller's shop and a hairdressing salon based on broken glass and portions of human anatomy set against a black background.

Fred rejects the Gothic label as hackneyed, though he admits that he finds the 'eeriness' of the Gothic style a stimulant. He describes his own style quite simply as 'emotional'. 'My idea is to generate an emotion because most design today is very static', he says.

'That is the idea of the whole room.' To Fred, life is inseparable from art and he states that 'art is what I try to create around me'.

Fred has transformed the sitting room by creating a platform to reduce the height of the walls and to turn the deep bay into a full length window. A dramatic glass sculpture and screen compensate for chain store furnishings.

Colin Fredricson's Design

Not surprisingly, Fred chose a radical design for Paul and Inger's living room. And if he didn't exactly raise the roof (rather difficult in a ground floor flat) he certainly lifted the floor.

His split level arrangement not only helps to create the maximum amount of space, but also adds style to a room which, in Fred's view, was 'bland and not very interesting'. By raising the sitting area, his intention was to add light to the space and 'give it more air'. 'High ceilings can be oppressive', explains Fred. 'A lower one makes you feel more relaxed.' Moreover, this scheme gave him the opportunity to use two separate types of flooring: velvet pile carpet on the platform, acknowledging Paul's request for quiet and comfort; and stripped floorboards on the lower area – a practical choice for what Fred envisaged as the dining area, and one that fulfilled Inger's request for wooden flooring.

Both sections of the room are decorated in neutral tones: the flooring is beige carpet or natural wood; the walls are sponged and ragged with grey on white, which gives a soft, cloudy effect, and white Venetian blinds cover the window. Paul's antiques add the warmth of dark timber; while the new, budget price furniture, which includes a sofabed, armchair, shelf units and glass topped coffee table, is all in black.

More extravagant are the optional 'accessories'. In the centre of the room a column of green glass, ending in a tongue of light (a snip at £9,000), undulates from floor to ceiling. In the chiselled-out chimney breast is a screen made from broken glass (a leitmotif of the Gothic style) set on black net and lit from behind via a dimmer switch to create a constant play of light. 'You won't need the telly with this to look at', says Fred, who concedes that these sculptures by Danny Lane are a luxury, but points out that they are not an essential part of the scheme.

Nor, to be frank, are Paul's antiques, which all three designers found difficult to integrate into their schemes. However, Fred's angst over this is most evident because he has

immortalized it in a painting of himself as Rodin's Thinker, seated on the chest while dismally pondering the corner cabinet. To emphasise the point, this self portrait is hung in the dining area right above the objects which caused him such despair. Yet, though at first sight they have little in common with the awe-inspiring stack of light, Fred believes that glass is a 'nostalgic' material which blends well with oak. Certainly the cupboard seems as much at home on the stripped floorboards as in a cottage, for which it was originally intended. And the sea chest has an affinity with the rippling screen, which recalls the movement of light on water.

The visual impact of this scheme fully justifies Fred's belief that changing the floor levels would produce a spacious, airy effect. By concentrating on neutral colours and sculptural accessories – including black obelisks,

white busts and a designer board game – Fred has created a restful atmosphere in which to contemplate the shining column or the shimmering screen. Take these away and you are left with a simple, budget price setting to relax in – and one which perhaps owes as much to the calm of the East as the gloom of Gothic.

Right. The chimney breast has been cut away to make room for a broken glass screen lit from within, which mirrors the effect of the tongue of light protruding from the green glass sculpture.

Below. In contrast to the carpeted platform, the original floor is sanded and sealed to make a practical dining area and to blend with the natural wood of the antique chest and cabinet.

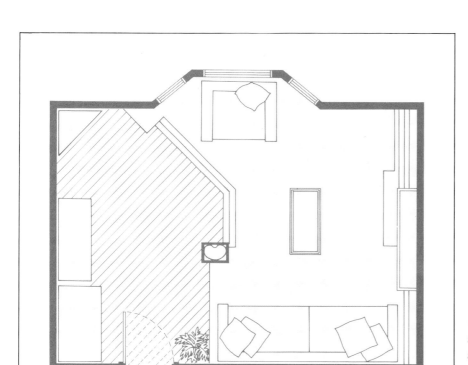

Fred's clever plan adds interest to a conventional suburban sitting room by creating a raised seating area cut in a wedge for an asymmetrical effect. The dining area has a practical sealed floor and is conveniently placed close to the entrance door.

Below. Diagonally placed steps and an undulating glass sculpture add a sense of excitement to the scheme and to help offset the regular shape of Paul and Inger's living room.

Left. Self Portrait of the Artist as a Despairing Young Man. The painting shows Fred seated disconsolately on the chest and pondering the corner cabinet while the pieces in question are ranged beneath.

Right. Fred's original sketch shows how faithfully he has translated his artist's impression into the room scheme. One minor change is the substitution of the glass tower for the tall column in the centre.

Black furniture and mottled grey walls provide a restrained setting which emphasises the effect of the flickering glass screen.

How to Sponge Walls

Sponging is one of the quickest and easiest of all the decorative paint techniques. Fred used it to great effect on the walls of the scheme he created for Paul and Inger's living room: producing a broken, mottled finish, much softer in appearance and more interesting to look at than a solid block of colour.

All you will need is a marine sponge about the size of your fist (don't use a synthetic one, as this will produce too uniform a print), a small dish and some paint. Eggshell is the most hardwearing, especially if there's steam about, but matt and silk vinyl emulsions are perfectly acceptable alternatives.

It is best to use muted shades – unless you have an unerring eye for colour – and to build up the finish with contrasting tonal overlays, rather than just one coat, to produce a more subtle, cloudy effect.

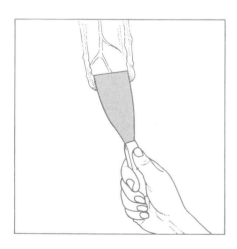

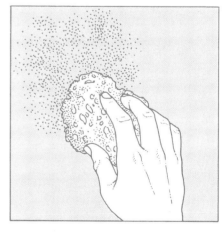

1 Prepare the surface to be decorated by washing down and rinsing to remove dust and grease. Fill any cracks and sand smooth, before applying two base coats of eggshell or emulsion in the colour of your choice.

2 Pour some of the paint for sponging into a dish (a saucer or roller tray will do), and thin with a little white spirit (if eggshell) or water (if emulsion). Dip the sponge into the dish and dab it onto a spare piece of paper several times to remove excess paint.

3 Sponge the paint over the base coat, using a dabbing and wrist-rolling action, to produce a mottled effect. Clean the sponge regularly to stop it becoming clogged and, if desired, apply a subtly contrasting colour on top when the first coat is dry, using the same method.

The Designer

3 Susy Smith

After leaving art college Susy Smith began her career working as a designer and stylist for various magazines. Nowadays she works as a freelance design consultant, interpreting the 'look of the moment' for clients who range from newspapers and magazines to chain stores and paint manufacturers.

As a stylist her job is to create room sets for advertisements and magazine features; that is, 'playing tricks' that turn three false walls and a few pieces of furniture into a 'real' room. In many ways life is easier for the stylist than the interior designer: 'we have a lot of freedom because we don't have the restrictions placed upon us by working in a normal room', acknowledges Susy. 'We can put the architectural details into a set ourselves, and light it the way we want.' On the other hand, Susy must have a very flexible attitude to style. For example, a magazine feature for first time buyers will require a very different approach to one aimed at an older and more affluent readership.

This chameleon-like quality is carried over into Susy's flair for colour and co-ordination. Her sets never include a cushion cover or lampshade which does not contribute to the overall effect, and her own home demonstrates the practical application of design ideas to the less than ideal reality of her dark basement kitchen/living room. Here, a warm sunshine yellow brightens up the walls, and is repeated in full curtains and a traditional sofa; whilst budget price units and woodwork are painted in a contrasting blue/grey. With her eye for detail, one bare brick chimney

breast is covered with bric-a-brac, ranging from purely decorative items to antique utensils and bunches of dried flowers.

Overall she has designed a cheerful, cost conscious and distinctively stylish interior – very like those depicted in the magazines Paul and Inger searched for inspiration.

Susy Smith's Design

£300 plus furnishings – that, according to Susy Smith, is the estimated cost of the living room, full of 'do it yourself' ideas, that she has designed for Paul and Inger.

The first decision Susy took was to restore the fireplace. 'I felt that the room badly needed a focal point, and the chimney breast was already there', she explains. The mantelpiece, with its delicate moulding, and the deep skirting and dado rail suggest an Edwardian style – which is echoed by the loose-covered sofa and wing chair (two classic designs which could easily be bought second hand, and re-covered to complement any scheme).

Although the room has a comfortable, old fashioned appeal Susy has relied heavily on a modern material, MDF (medium density fibreboard), for the construction of the occasional table, plinths, box shelving, cupboards, and mantelpiece. Because it is low cost, stable and 'wonderful to paint because it's so smooth', MDF is ideal for DIY.

Even the decorative urns are simply terracotta garden pots painted to repeat the room's dominant colours. 'Accessories are terribly important in a room', says Susy. 'I felt it was crucial to pull out the colours on the wall and distribute them elsewhere – in the

Although it is more decorative than Paul and Inger's original decor, Susy's light and airy scheme seems to increase the impression of space. Paint treatments and DIY furniture made from medium density fibreboard contribute to this budget-price setting which combines economy and style.

cushions, lampshades, various pieces of china and so on.' This helps to create a fully co-ordinated scheme which adds light and warmth to the room.

One difficulty, as Susy admits, is that the pastel colours contrast strongly with the dark oak of Paul and Inger's antique furniture. To bring this into the scheme, Susy has moved the sea chest to beneath the bay window, and given it an apricot coloured cushion to provide additional seating and match the curtain tie-backs and pelmet above; the corner cupboard is where its name suggests, and is partially obscured by the end of the sofa and a plinth to minimize its presence.

The floor-length curtains at the bay window are made from ticking (another budget price material), and privacy is provided by Roman blinds made from silk noil (a surprisingly economic choice as well as a stylish one) – 'I always think nets look so ugly', says Susy. Other natural fibres are found in the heavy cotton upholstery and the wool dhurry in which the scheme's apricot, blue and cream colours combine. The rug fulfils Paul's request for comfort and warmth; whilst the surrounding floorboards are sanded and varnished to satisfy Inger's wish for a natural wood floor.

Space-saving ideas are important in a room this size, so Susy devised a dual-purpose table; the top is set on low supports for television suppers and coffee, but for more formal meals it can be placed over the lower sections of the two columns by the window (they both split neatly in two). This creates a table exactly at the right height for dining, yet still leaves two plinths for the table lamps. Folding chairs, brought in from the kitchen, would complete the transition from living to dining room.

Finally, one of the cupboards to the side of the fireplace conceals the video and television, which swings out on a support bracket; the other hides the music centre. 'I often hide them away because they're not particularly nice unless you're living in a high-tech environment', says Susy, whose sense of style keeps technology firmly in its place.

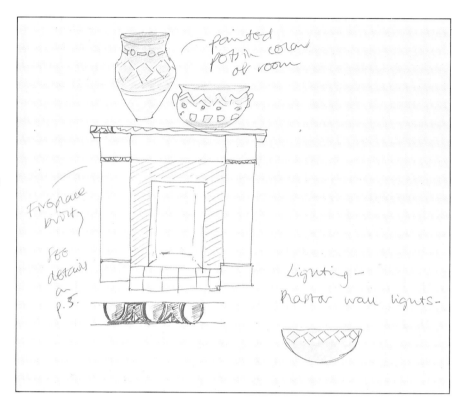

Top. Susy's sketch shows how she has painted the mantelpiece and terracotta pots to complement her scheme.

Above. The ingenious table is set on low plinths for everyday use, but can be raised on the table lamp columns to dining height.

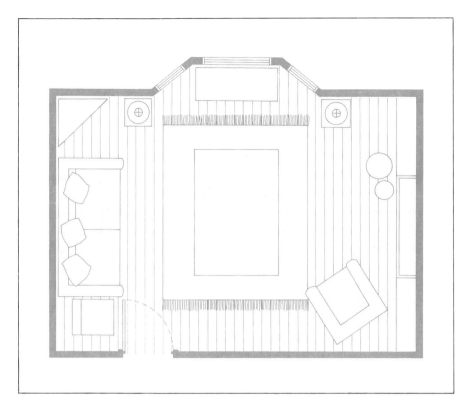

Susy's plan is simple and symmetrical to make the most of space. The new mantelpiece and shelves cover the chimney breast wall and a small sofa is ranged opposite. Additional seating is provided by the wing chair and a cushion which tops the sea chest in the window bay.

Below. MDF or medium density fibreboard is a smooth material which is cheap and easy to paint. It looks just as effective used for a traditional mantelpiece as for modern furniture and can be repainted when necessary to suit a change of scheme. Susy has chosen a bright and sunny colour combination of apricot and blue.

The tall columns which support the lamps split neatly in two, providing plinths which turn the occasional table into one for dining as well as alternative low stands for the lights.

How to Paint a Striped Finish

Painting a striped wall finish, as Susy Smith has done in Paul and Inger's living room, is a simple project that provides a cheaper and more durable finish than wallpaper. Obviously you can choose your own combination of colours, and as the striped areas will be defined by masking tape, you won't need a steady hand.

Susy has opted for vertical stripes to counter the dado and visually heighten the room. But you can use horizontal stripes if you wish, remembering that they will 'lower' the ceiling.

The colours of the stripes should be related (such as apricot and pale yellow or blue/grey and lilac) for a restful setting; and complementary or contrasting (such as blue/grey and apricot or pink and green) for a livelier look.

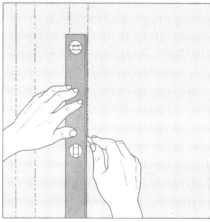

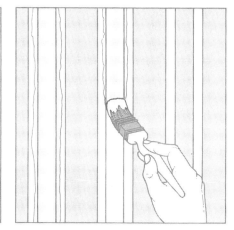

1 Clean all dirt and grease from the wall. Repair any cracks, and sand smooth when filler has dried. If the surface was previously gloss or eggshell painted (as opposed to papered), rub down with wet and dry paper. Prime the walls if painting on to bare plaster.

2 Apply two coats of emulsion or eggshell paint to the entire surface of the walls. This should be the lighter of the two colours you have chosen. When dry, mark out the sides of the stripes using a long spirit level and a piece of soft chalk – their width is a matter of personal preference.

3 Carefully fix low-tack masking tape down both sides of the stripes. Apply two coats of the darker colour in the panels between the tape, so that the base coat is obliterated. When the paint is dry, very carefully remove the masking tape to reveal the striped finish.

Paul and Inger's Conclusion

Paul and Inger were taken with Fred's scheme, especially the raised platform which Inger thought 'had a Japanese effect, and gave the room a character it sorely lacked' – though she felt it could still do with some primary colours. Paul was less certain about the glass sculpture, and wanted to add the shelves and winged chair from Susy's scheme. However, Inger thought Susy's look 'too contrived', though it 'brought a glow into the room'.

Paul preferred the 'clean lines' of David Hicks' design, especially the window treatment and furniture. He thought this would be the most flexible, because 'you could add objects without feeling you had interrupted the mood'.

So, it would seem Paul and Inger's room may eventually include a raised platform, traditional cupboards and chairs, geometric curtains and bright colours – quite a novel and stimulating mixture.

THE
KITCHEN

The popularity of kitchen planning services testifies to the fact that this is the room people find most difficult to design. Perhaps they are mystified by the 'science' of kitchen planning, or feel unqualified to resolve technical questions concerning plumbing and electricity. Whatever the cause, the result is that kitchen replacement is a boom industry.

That's good news for the kitchen companies, and for householders who can afford the £5000-plus a dream kitchen can cost. But sometimes the budget won't stretch that far and indeed, not everyone likes the rather uniform look of rows of mass-produced fitted units. So, what help is there for those who neither want nor can afford a kitchen straight from the manufacturer's brochure?

There are several principles of design which may enable you to plan your kitchen without expert help. The first is to establish a 'work triangle' which links together the fridge and food preparation area with the cooker and sink. In an average size U-shaped or L-shaped kitchen this is best achieved via unbroken expanses of worktop. However, this is not possible in a long, narrow room, where all the appliances have to be sited along one wall (an 'in-line' kitchen); or in a small galley kitchen, where units and appliances have to be placed on opposite sides. Surprisingly, very large kitchens can be equally awkward to plan because the usual backs-to-the-wall arrangement for units and appliances may involve unwanted exercise for the cook. In this case the usual solution is to restrict the size of the work triangle, by providing an island unit to bring the cooker and cupboards closer together.

As you will see, none of these systems or types of kitchen could be directly implemented in the Whardles' home. Instead, you will find echoes of all of them in our designers' schemes, as well as a complete disregard for them – as with most kitchens, the difficulty of the layout meant that some compromises had to be made.

THE ORIGINAL KITCHEN

Debra Whardle, with her husband Misha and their two children Jason and Kitty, recently moved into a maisonette above Misha's picture framing shop. Business is good, and although Misha has little time to think about redecorating, Debra, who enjoys cooking, would like some advice on the layout of their new kitchen.

'It's virtually impossible to work in my kitchen', wailed Debra Whardle. 'It's small, awkward, the cupboards are in the wrong place and because I'm only 5ft tall I have to stand on a chair to reach them.'

Certainly her kitchen was minute, the size of the average utility room – with the difference that Debra had to cram a cooker, sink and units in a galley arrangement along one wall. The one compensation was that it led off a large, sunny dining room with french windows opening on to a roof terrace.

Unfortunately, Debra's attempts to add a touch of style to the dining room, which included adding a stencilled frieze, were being undermined by the overspill from the kitchen. This included a freezer, a microwave, a fridge and the use of the dining table for food preparation – inconvenient in view of the cooker's location.

Storage space was another problem, being confined to a few tacky kitchen units and a cupboard in the dining room. The lighting was equally poor, consisting of just two pendant lights, and the heating was supplied by a rather ugly gas fire. Not surprisingly Debra decided it was time for a change.

She wanted an efficient kitchen and a family dining room, with sufficient seating for six to eight (retaining her existing dining table and chairs if possible). The only existing appliance to be retained was the freestanding microwave. But somehow a new oven, separate gas hob, fridge, freezer, washing machine and, if possible, dishwasher had to be squeezed in, along with the usual kitchen paraphernalia. She was happy to get rid of the old kitchen units, but was anxious to keep within a budget of £2500, excluding appliances.

In addition, she wanted to make a feature of the french windows leading on to the terrace (where her three year old, Kitty, plays). She was open to suggestions about the overall style – though expressed a preference for pastel colours and a distaste for carpet. However, she also wanted to recall her home country of Jamaica, where the kitchen is the centre of the home. 'In the West Indies cookers are usually larger and the floor is normally tiled. There's a fan overhead, so it's very airy and the atmosphere is very relaxed.' Could the designers convey that in Debra's cramped suburban kitchen?

You can see from this plan of the Whardles' kitchen why Debra was so desperate for expert help. The kitchen itself is little more than galley size, which means that the freezer, fridge, microwave, table and chairs all occupy the breakfast room. This has a pleasant outlook and leads on to an attractive roof terrace where Kitty plays, but in terms of kitchen planning, simply creates another doorway to interrupt the flow of units.

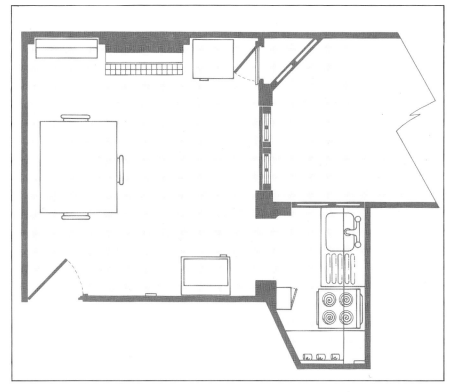

Above. High storage cupboards, a sink unit and cooker are crammed into a wedge-shaped room that's little bigger than a broom cupboard.

Right. The dining room looks on to a sunny terrace formed by the roof of the studio where husband Misha works.

Left. Lack of storage space means that ironing board and freezer jostle for position by the tiny wall larder.

The Designer

I Roy Ackerman

As a kitchen designer, Roy Ackerman has one undoubted qualification: he is passionately interested in food. He loves to cook and believes one should 'live to eat rather than eat to live'.

This lifelong affair with food may have left its mark on his figure, but has also influenced his rise in the hierarchy from *commis chef* to chairman of the Restaurateurs' Association of Great Britain. He is also deputy chairman of the Kennedy Brookes empire of one hundred restaurants and hotels, ranging from Wheeler's traditional English fish restaurants, via Mario and Franco trattorias to the Bear Hotel in Woodstock.

Often Roy's work involves catering on the grand scale (feeding two thousand at the Chelsea Arts Ball or eight thousand at Henley, for example). But his private entertaining is a more modest affair – serving twenty to twenty five guests at a time with 'robust and exotic' meals in the cavernous space of the converted Fulham car parts factory which he has made his home.

The open plan arrangement of this building is ideal for a cook who, while seriously devoted to the task, is also a *bon viveur* who likes to mingle with his guests – 'food is an art form', says Roy. This explains why his kitchens (he has one upstairs, and one down) are functional, while the open plan living room and dining areas that lead off them are embellished with theatrical Tuscan arches, screens, palms, plaster busts and objets d'art.

'The kitchen is the focal point of the house as far as I'm concerned', he declares. 'And have you noticed how

all the best parties seem to end up in the kitchen?' Beliefs that were to stand him in good stead when planning the Whardles' kitchen.

Roy Ackerman brings a touch of the tropics, complete with ceiling fan, to the Whardles' suburban kitchen.

Roy Ackerman's Design

Debra Whardle's preference for a kitchen which would be an expression of her personality and the centre of her home was in complete accord with Roy Ackerman's own ideas.

The most striking feature of his dramatic design is the marbled panelled bar. This is a dramatic, attractive yet practical way of integrating the process of food preparation into the living and dining area, allowing Debra to enjoy the company of her family or guests, as well as providing hidden storage space for kitchen equipment.

Although Roy likes to prepare food standing up ('it's the only way', he says) he has provided two tall bentwood stools should Debra prefer to sit down, and for snack meals at the bar. The rest of the seating consists of the original dining table, chairs and a new bench seat, thus fulfilling the request that the dining area should be able to cater for six to eight guests.

However, the 'business end' of the kitchen has been planned with just one person in mind. The space behind the bar is limited, allowing just enough room for the cook to turn round to reach the worktop, shelves, hob and oven – the latter fitted in a staggered arrangement for safety, so that the cook's hair will not be scorched on the hob when opening the oven. The original galley kitchen has been converted to a utility room. ('It keeps the dirty work out of the way', explains Roy.) Inside are plain units for extra storage, the sink, washing machine, microwave and fridge. The freezer remains in the dining area, but is now cleverly concealed in the old storage cupboard, which has been enlarged to project onto the patio.

In terms of style, the whole scheme reflects Debra Whardle's taste and background. By using pastel shades and flashes of bold colour, offset by traditional, white table linen, Roy has created a theatrical setting with a feeling of warmth and a sense of space. Thus the soft mango and pink of the walls and bar; the stencilled tropical fruit frieze, which spills off the walls onto the roller blind; the bamboo style lamp; the ceiling fan; the earthenware mugs; paintings enlarged from postcards of the Caribbean and the profusion of houseplants.

Costs were kept down (the entire kitchen came to just under £2000) by using cheap or salvaged furnishings, but embellishing them with elegant, decorative paint treatments – most notable being the marbled bar and the 'fossilised' units behind it (see 'how to create a marbled finish', page 35). Similarly, the stencilled frieze is a cheap and easy way to add a touch of individuality (see 'how to stencil a frieze', page 34). The only extravagant item, at £450, was the Amtico vinyl tile floor, laid with a border to emphasise the shape of the bar. However, Roy points out that a simple and cheaper alternative would be to paint the boards in a similar fashion, and varnish them for protection.

Roy hopes this kitchen is a place where the Whardles and their guests will feel happy and relaxed. He concedes that it has a sense of theatre 'but why not? I'm a showman, not a professional designer', he says. 'I want to get people interested in food.'

Right. Behind the bar, which concedes the storage cupboards, are the oven and hob and all the equipment needed for food preparation.

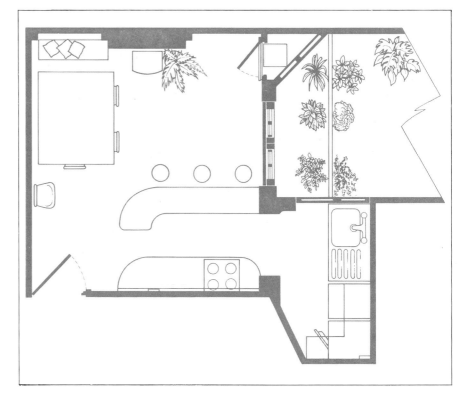

The marbled bar ingeniously links the breakfast room with the original kitchen, but allows clear access to the french windows and roof terrace. A new seating unit at the end of the existing dining table provides the extra seating required.

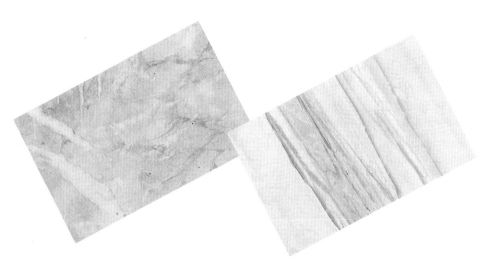

Left. Marbling in white and rose quartz colours creates a convincing trompe l'oeil effect on the plywood used for the bar.

Below. Bright colour is concentrated in the accessories and frieze, while warm pastels create an impression of space.

How to Stencil a Frieze

A stencilled frieze, like the one Roy Ackerman painted for the Whardles' kitchen, is an inexpensive and simple way to introduce visual interest, colour and a touch of individuality.

For a first attempt it would be best to buy a book of ready-cut stencils.

There are plenty of designs to choose from – birds, flowers, animals, abstract patterns, etc. With a little patience you will achieve very 'professional' results. Having gained some experience, if you are prepared to cut your own stencils you will be able to create a co-ordinated scheme by repeating motifs used on fabrics, tiles and other

items elsewhere in the room.

You will need stencil card (acetate or Mylar is best), a craft knife, low-tack masking tape, a stencil brush (available from artists' suppliers), a chinagraph pencil and any kind of paint – Roy used poster paint – provided its appearance when dry is compatible with the rest of the wall.

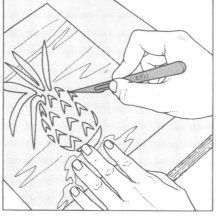

1 Place the clear acetate or Mylar over your design, and trace the outlines onto it with a pencil. Leave a 5cm (2inch) margin around the edge for strength during cutting. If the picture or pattern is large or complicated you may need to make a separate stencil for each section.

2 Place a board underneath, and cut around the outlines with a craft knife. Leave strips ('bridges') of the acetate intact, to separate areas of different colour and detail. The bridges should be approximately 3mm ($\frac{1}{8}$ inch) wide.

3 Having marked out the intended course of the frieze, fix the stencil(s) in position on the wall with low-tack masking tape. Apply the paint with a stencil brush, using a dabbing action. Don't overload the brush, and stick to one colour at a time.

4 When the paint has dried, carefully remove the stencil and reposition it for the next section of the frieze . . . and so on. You may wish to invert the stencil alternately to create a more flowing look. Finish with a protective coat of polyurethane varnish.

How to Create a Marbled Finish

As the splendid bar Roy Ackerman designed for the Whardles' kitchen shows, the main virtue of marbling is that it enables you to convert cheap components such as MDF (medium density fibreboard) units and doors into seemingly expensive and luxurious fittings.

The essence of this decorative technique is to capture the essential qualities of marble, rather than reproduce it in detail. However it is a good idea to use a piece or picture of marble for reference.

You will need: a 'swordliner' brush, a hog's hair softener and blender, artists' oils, scumble glaze (all available from artists' suppliers), eggshell paint, white spirit, a lint-free rag, varnish and a standard 5cm (2 inch) paint brush. Start by practising on a piece of board, before tackling the kitchen units and worktop.

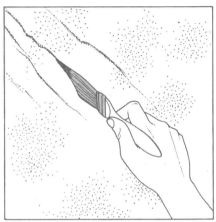

1 Fill, rub down and clean the surface in the normal way. Then prime with two coats of a pale coloured eggshell paint. When dry, brush on a glaze of 50% eggshell/ 20% white spirit/30% scumble, and dab it with a lint-free rag to produce a soft, cloudy effect.

2 To represent the veins, apply artists' oils (use a darker colour than the primer coat) diagonally across the surface, using a fine 'swordliner'. Vary their thickness and add a network of finer secondary veins. Throughout, refer to your piece or picture of marble for inspiration.

3 Before they dry, dab the veins with a hog's hair softener and blender. This will produce a mottled effect and make them appear to lie just beneath the surface of the 'stone'. When dry, apply several coats of matt or satin finish polyurethane varnish.

Left. Roy has enlarged prints from Caribbean postcards to complement the frieze and to reflect Debra's origins.

Right. No one would guess that this 'marble' bar is actually painted plywood. Subtle hues were used; see technique above.

The Designer

2 Pedro Guedes

Portugal and Africa have had an equally strong influence on the work of architect Pedro Guedes, born to Portuguese parents and brought up in Mozambique. Though his heritage is revealed by the ornate dark woods and carvings which decorate the kitchen of his own home in Tufnell Park, London, the most eye-catching features of this room are an expression of his own unorthodox style.

Stained glass, burning tapers (flames are a leitmotif of his work), and a vast hardwood pediment, which forms the apex of what in any other setting would be called kitchen units, turn his kitchen into a cathedral. Whether it is a temple to the art of cooking is open to question – Pedro admits to buying groceries on the strength of their packaging as much as for the nutritional merits of their contents.

What is undeniable is that thanks to his pragmatic approach to design, these grand ideas required only the smallest of budgets. In fact, his entire kitchen is a monument to architectural salvage; for Pedro, a skip brimming with junk is a source of inspiration, believing that natural materials age more gracefully (he has an aversion to laminates), even if they do need major surgery. Thus his kitchen rests, quite literally, on three Victorian sideboards, which serve as the base units; an Edwardian hallstand serves as a plate rack, a car fender is adapted to decorate an extractor fan and old bedlegs adorn a spice rack.

So, it is evident that while the principles of architectural and interior design are important to Pedro he doesn't think they should be taken too seriously. Or rather, they shouldn't be

slavishly followed to the point where individuality is stifled. This is why he is very much against mass-produced fitted kitchens, feeling that people should be given as much encouragement as possible to personalise their own homes.

Above. An unusual kitchen that 'breaks all the rules of kitchen planning' is Pedro's solution to the Whardles' dilemma.

Pedro Guedes' Design

Pedro Guedes' intention to 'preserve the separate character' of the Whardles' kitchen and dining room involved dividing food preparation and cooking into two distinct areas, thereby dispensing with the 'work triangle' – one of the lynch pins of conventional kitchen planning.

The original galley kitchen, tiled in white and furnished with plain white shelving and a worktop, houses the 'messy appliances' such as the sink, washing machine and hob, and is concealed from the dining room by double doors. There are no cupboards or drawers. Instead, the area serves as a 'garage' for two trolleys, used to transport vegetables, laundry, dirty dishes etc between the two areas.

In contrast with this simplicity, the dining area is dominated by a purpose-made dresser, in a flamboyant post-modern style, flanked by twin cabinets containing the oven and fridge-freezer. The intention is that this should form a serving unit, keeping china and food that's ready to eat close to the dining area. Concentrating the units on one wall leaves plenty of space for the Whardles' original dining table and chairs, and allows easy access to the roof terrace.

The dresser and units are made from MDF (medium density fibreboard), which Pedro estimates cost £600, and are topped by a real granite worktop – at around £20 a foot the one luxury Pedro has allowed. The design was chosen especially to reflect Misha Whardle's trade (he is a picture framer), the units being clad in panels cut to form frames for the dozens of tiny coloured squares beneath (see 'how to panel doors', page 41). It is a deliberate mix of the decorative and the practical – mirrors, plants and prints taking their place on the dresser beside the pulses, spice jars and kitchen tools. There is even an ironing board that folds out from above one of the drawer units.

Although the new kitchen is decorated in the pastels Debra favoured, Pedro has arranged them on the units to form a striking colour scheme in which white and grey surfaces are spattered with a profusion of soft pink, red, yellow, black and blue. By way of contrast, the walls are quite plain, being painted a sunny yellow colour, though Pedro has added a plate rack for decorative china at picture rail height. This adds visual interest and helps to keep the height of the central dresser unit in proportion to the rest of the room. Finally, the floor is covered with sealed cork tiles, which are warm, resilient and washable.

The result is a dramatic scheme which Pedro feels the Whardles could personalise, if they wished, by framing favourite pictures inside the larger coloured panels of the units.

Above. Food preparation is consigned to the original kitchen where trolleys transport it to the main cooking and serving area.

Right. The dresser which dominates the room also encloses oven, fridge/freezer and ironing board.

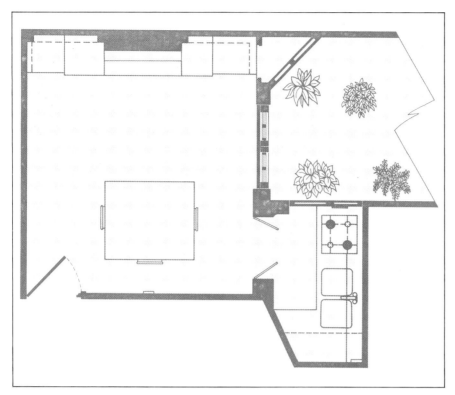

Pedro has divided the kitchen into two distinct areas: one for the messy work of washing up and food preparation (which also includes cooking on the hob), the other, housed in the magnificent cabinet, catering for long-term cooking (hence the built-in oven), and storage for food, china and ironing equipment.

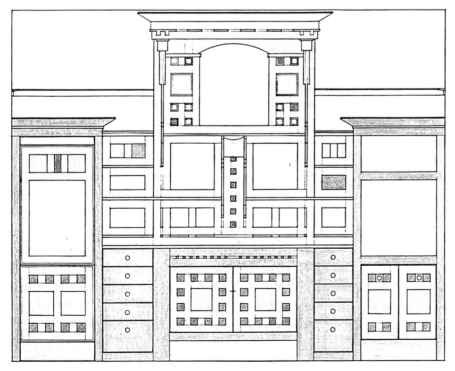

The huge kitchen dresser is the centrepiece of Pedro's design, incorporating storage units, an oven, fridge and even ironing board behind decorative panelled doors. His tinted sketch (left) shows careful asymmetry in his colouring of the panels, creating an effect that is both unusual and pleasing to the eye.

How to Panel Doors

The elaborate dresser that Pedro Guedes created for the Whardles is a variation of the one in his own kitchen. However, while his was created from three Victorian sideboards, which are features in their own right, the Whardles' units are constructed from MDF, a functional material not known for its aesthetic qualities.

Many of our designers have used MDF in their schemes, and cleverly disguised it with various exciting paint techniques. However, Pedro has used an ingenious combination of colour and carpentry to embellish his construction. Thin strips of MDF have been stuck to the flat surface of the doors, to form raised frames around dozens of tiny squares painted in contrasting colours. This simple technique is an ideal way of making new doors that appear to be constructed on traditional lines, and also a way of revamping old ones.

1 Secure a piece of MDF on a workbench and, using a powered circular saw, cut out strips for the frame – their width is a matter of personal preference. If you do not have access to these tools, most timber yards will cut out the strips to your specification.

2 Measure the top, bottom and sides of the door you wish to frame, and cut strips of MDF to the required length. If you have decided to stain rather than paint the frame (as a contrast to the painted centre section), use soft or hardwood strips instead, and stain them now.

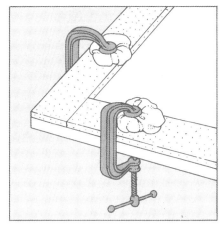

3 Assemble the door frame by securing the strips in position with an impact adhesive such as Evo-Stik. Hold them in place with G-clamps, padded with cloth, while the glue dries. Thicker strips of soft and hardwood can also be secured from the back with wood screws.

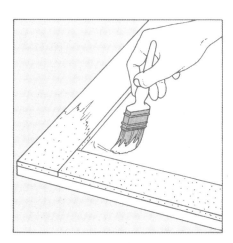

4 Key the now framed door for painting and apply two coats of wood primer. (Obviously this does not apply to previously stained soft or hardwood strips.)

5 Protect the centre section of the door with low-tack masking tape, and paint the MDF frame with two coats of eggshell finish paint in the colour of your choice. (Again, this will not apply to a previously stained frame.) Allow to dry.

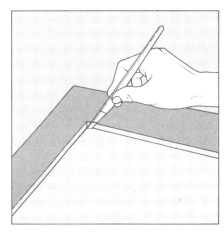

6 Remove the masking tape and paint the centre section of the door with two coats of a contrasting eggshell colour. Use a fine angled window brush to carefully paint into the corners and around the edges.

The Designer

Lynn Davis

3 Lynn Davis

Designing for small spaces is second nature to Lynn Davis. Her company, Lynn Davis Architects, specialises in developing the awkward infill sites between existing buildings – often the only ground left for new offices and homes in London and the south-east.

Lynn's own award-winning office, built in a disused builder's yard in Holland Park, is an angled steel construction, which depends on the clever use of glass to make the most of limited natural light. Most of her projects are commercial studios and offices which she oversees, taking advantage of her husband's building expertise, from planning stage to completion.

Her own home – one of three in a converted school – demonstrates her flair for domestic interiors, and the simple decor, designed to reflect the character of the building, reveals her architectural background. The walls are either painted or bare brick and the floor is covered with French provincial tiles. Natural materials are used again in the kitchen units, where veneered and solid ash doors disguise basic MFI carcasses, and echo the pale pink and honey tones of the walls. The worktop is a particular favourite of Lynn's, made from standard lengths of bleached beech, glued and screwed together and oiled for protection.

Her kitchen is part of an open plan ground floor – an arrangement which suits Lynn because, like Debra Whardle, she feels the kitchen should be part of the living area. 'If I'm cooking, I don't like to feel as if I'm down the corridor', she says, preferring an environment where

guests can meander in and out, talk and have a drink.

However, while Lynn believes she has designed the appropriate style for her own kitchen and home, she thinks it wouldn't be quite right for the Whardles. 'I intend to use a different finish that's more appropriate to Debra, and more colourful and more urban.'

Right. Now extended outwards, the room has swallowed up the galley kitchen to create a regular shape. The outside terrace is now easily accessible from the kitchen and dining area, and the glass door and new skylight provides an important source of natural light.

Below. The dramatic paint finish on the central units in Lynn's kitchen makes it an important visual centrepiece.

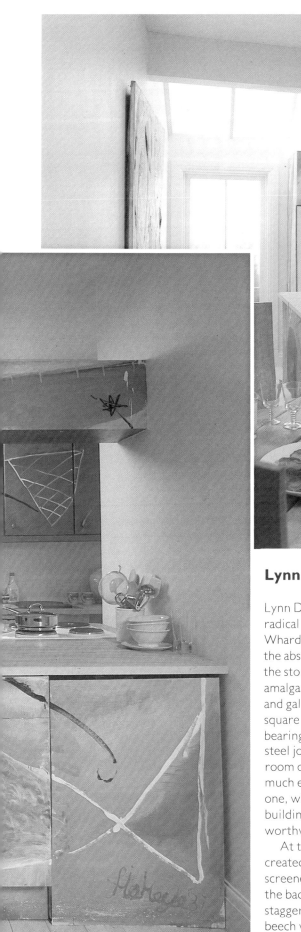

Lynn Davis' Design

Lynn Davis' design was the most radical of the three schemes for the Whardles' kitchen. Quite apart from the abstract painting, which utilises the storage units as a canvas, she has amalgamated the separate dining area and galley kitchen into one large, square room, by replacing a load-bearing wall with an RSJ (reinforced steel joist) and extending the dining room onto the terrace. This layout is much easier to equip than the original one, which Lynn feels makes the building costs (about £2500) well worthwhile.

At the rear of the new room she created an open plan kitchen, but screened it from the dining area with the back of the oven housing, staggered shelving, storage units and beech worktop. The units are embellished with a mural which

features the outline of a fish with one pink eye fixed, quite literally, on the left hand door knob. Appropriately, the mural conceals the washing machine and tumble dryer (the 'wet wall' appliances), plus an ironing board. Lynn makes a point of separating the laundry and food preparation areas, the rationale being that 'nothing is worse than finding dirty washing among the cooking'!

Behind these units, in the kitchen proper, is a compact galley arrangement which houses the split level oven and hob, dishwasher, microwave and fridge-freezer, which Debra had specified. Lynn is very keen on the idea of 'circular motion with lots of put down space' (a development of the 'work triangle' principle), and always plans her kitchens in this logical way. The sequence starts with food storage, moves to the sink, where it is washed, and progresses to the areas for preparation, cooking and serving – a dishwasher being fitted, where possible, to complete the cycle.

As is her usual practice, Lynn has used standard chipboard carcasses for the units, but the doors are far removed from the conventional melamine or wood veneer finish. 'I want people to use paint finishes, not plain laminate', she says, suggesting paint straight from the tin, or stencilled or marbled effects as easier alternatives to the abstract mural her specialist painter created for the Whardles. Though she urges householders to approach students at the local art school, if they want a truly original finish!

By confining the units to one side of the room, the roof terrace can be reached without having to cross the kitchen area; an important safety point where there are small children around. For reasons of space the french windows have been replaced by a glazed panelled door, and skylights built in to compensate for the reduced natural light.

Colours are cool, with white walls, grey and white units and the blue of the mural offset by touches of pink and yellow. The beech worktop is matched with a light, wooden strip floor, and Lynn has substituted a modern, light wood dining table and four chairs for the Whardles' original furniture.

The price of change? At about £2,500–£3,000, including appliances, it is within the Whardles' budget, but of course that does not include the initial £2,500 for structural alterations.

Above right. This pull-out ironing board is designed to solve the usual problems of storage and accessibility.

Lynn's plan is the most ambitious of the three kitchen designs. To overcome the problem of the awkward kitchen, she suggests extending the breakfast room on to the terrace and demolishing the walls which divide the two rooms to form a large rectangle that is easy to equip.

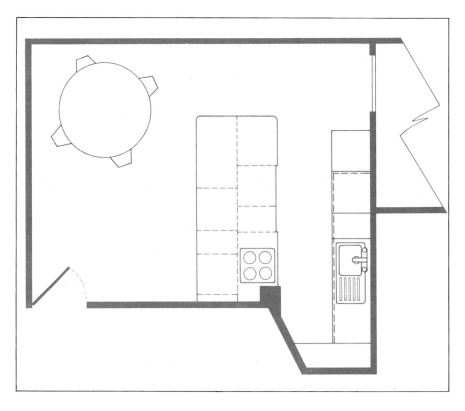

Top right. The abstract painting makes a splash on the cupboards.

Below right. The double oven is built into a column to disguise it from the dining area.

Below. The inventors of this 'pop-out' board applied gas lift principles to power the smooth movement out of the cupboard. Because the board is attached to a single stalk, it can turn 360° and so ironing becomes instantly easier.

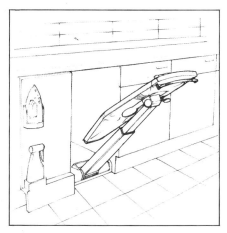

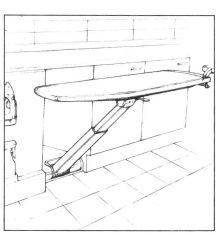

How to Prepare Kitchen Units for a New Paint Finish

Perhaps the most striking feature of the kitchen Lynn Davis designed for the Whardles is the colourful abstract mural that enhances the new storage units. Such a dramatic effect need not be confined to a new kitchen. Indeed,

Lynn recommends using the technique as a way of transforming your old one without the inconvenience and cost of replacing the original units.

Moreover, if you feel such a mural is beyond your artistic abilities then a marbled, sponged, stencilled, distressed, sprayed or straightforward painted finish can be equally effective.

However, the presence of steam and widely fluctuating temperatures in a kitchen requires that any surface to be painted is diligently prepared and the finish is sufficiently protected. This is especially important if you are working on old melamine or laminate faced units.

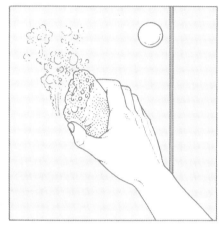

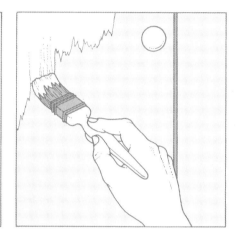

1 Wash down melamine, laminates and varnished surfaces with a solution of sugar soap, to remove dust, dirt and grease. Rinse thoroughly and allow to dry. With stripped wood, neutralise chemical stripper with acetic acid (vinegar) and remove dirt with white spirit.

2 To key the surface for paint, rub down bare wood with fine grade sandpaper. Melamine and laminate surfaces, being smooth, hard and designed to withstand scratching, must be rubbed down thoroughly with wet fine grade silicon carbide paper (wet and dry), rinsed and left to dry.

3 Prime all bare wood with two coats of wood primer, and prime melamine, laminates or varnished wood with oil-based eggshell paint. Protect the finished article with two coats of matt or silk polyurethane varnish, rubbing down with fine grade wet and dry paper between coats. If you wish to avoid varnishing, Lynn suggests simply using a spray can of enamel paint – this can be used on plastics, and has an attractive high sheen.

Debra's Conclusion

Debra liked the layout of Lynn's scheme best of all, though she was less enthusiastic about the painting. She admired Pedro's custom-built dresser, but found the colours overpowering, and felt she couldn't cope with the way he had divided up the space. She settled on a combination of Roy's kitchen, which she especially approved for its pleasant colour scheme, unusual paint treatments and its attention to her budget, and Lynn's layout, adapted to incorporate a bar – this time topped with real marble!

THE DINING ROOM

Everyone knows there is a difference between a snack eaten to keep body and soul together and a meal served as a celebration. Indeed, it's precisely because a sense of occasion can be difficult to achieve when eating in the kitchen or living area that a separate dining room is still popular, despite today's more relaxed lifestyles and despite the demands it can make on living space.

Few dining rooms are large enough to serve a dual purpose, because the table and chairs occupy most of the floor area (though the table makes an ideal surface for sewing). Consequently, most become 'something of a showcase' – which is how one government-sponsored survey described the attitude of homeowners to them. In many affluent homes you will find the classic furniture, bone china, silver and crystal displayed in the traditional dining room. However, it is not necessary to possess or buy such valuable items to create a stunning setting. For example, a door supported on trestles and covered with sheeting makes an imposing table, while basic garden chairs can be painted or stained a co-ordinating colour. And inexpensive, elegant white earthenware can be used to supplement miscellaneous pieces of 'best' bone china and tableware.

In some respects, decorating a dining room demands a theatrical instinct. As you will be using the room for relatively short periods of time, it is possible to be more adventurous than with some of the other rooms in the home, where a dramatic decor may soon pall. So, experiment with tented ceilings, dark colours, mood lighting and ambitious paint techniques and, if you're looking for inspiration and guidance, take a look at the problems our three designers faced and the solutions they came up with. But whatever the scheme you decide on, don't forget to make the table the focal point of any formal meal to provide a feast for the eyes whatever the standard of cooking.

THE ORIGINAL DINING ROOM

Roger MacLaverty, a solicitor, and his wife Christine Browning, a hospital manager, live with their two young daughters in their Edwardian home. They take a keen interest in interior design, but are unsure how to incorporate their collection of pictures, objets d'art and china.

'I would like a room which makes people say "This is amazing!"', declared Christine Browning, briefing the designers on her dining room. But the room had to be more than eye-catching. It needed to cater for six to eight guests, include a place for serving dishes and, most importantly, incorporate and reflect Christine and husband Roger's prize possession; an Art Deco dinner service by Clarice Cliff, depicting scenes of flappers and their escorts enjoying a pre-war cruise in a lighthearted, flirtatious and sometimes distinctly saucy way.

Christine and Roger are indefatigable collectors, and their home in Kingston is crowded with prints and objets d'art. They have made a special study of Art Deco china and own an impressive collection of jugs, but the immaculate blue and white Cruiseware service takes pride of place. It is too valuable to eat from so they have no intention of ever using it but simply want to display it to its full effect.

Another problem was the chimney breast. A rectangular recess was all that remained to mark the position of the original fireplace. But, Christine and Roger couldn't decide whether to install another, in suitable Edwardian style, fill in the cavity to provide extra wall space, or simply use the recess in an interesting and constructive way.

In addition: they wondered how to reconcile the Edwardian style of the room, with its delightful north and south facing windows, with the Art Deco of their dinner service; they couldn't decide whether or not to replace their late Victorian furniture with a something more in keeping with the age of the flapper; they were unsure whether to strip the floorboards, which were solid and in good condition, or to cover them with tiles or carpet, and finally, they needed advice about a more effective lighting system.

Christine and Roger had pondered these problems for two years and together had reached an impasse. With plaster peeling in patches from the walls, and the Clarice Cliff still in a packing case, they felt it was time to bring in an expert to unite the conflicting elements and create a distinctive dining room.

OPPOSITE. THE GRACEFUL PROPORTIONS OF THE ROOM AND ITS FINE WINDOWS ARE MARRED BY AN UNINTERESTING SCHEME WHICH DOES NOTHING TO EMPHASISE ITS ARCHITECTURAL FEATURES, AND BY THE EMPTY SPACE WHICH MARKS THE POSITION OF THE ORIGINAL FIREPLACE.

LEFT. ALTHOUGH THEY HAD STRIPPED ONE WALL OF THE DINING ROOM IN THEIR EDWARDIAN HOME, CHRISTINE AND ROGER WERE UNABLE TO DECIDE ON A SUITABLE SCHEME. COULD ROOM FOR CHANGE HELP?

The original room contains the bare minimum of furniture that a dining room requires. Christine and Roger have nowhere to display their collection of paintings, or the valuable Clarice Cliff dinner service they want to incorporate in the scheme.

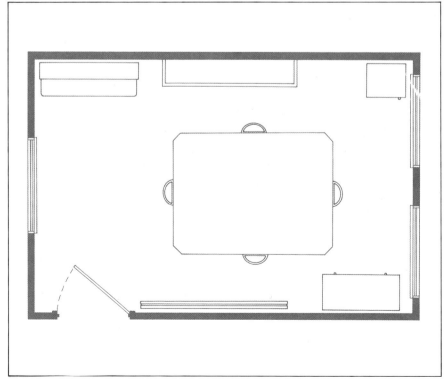

The Designer

1   Cebuan de la Rochette

Franco-Italian parentage and a cosmopolitan background is reflected in the exotic quality of Cebuan de la Rochette's work as a flower arranger and sculptor. Equally influential is the Far East, especially India, where she 'fell in love with colour', and Japan, the source of *ikebana*, an artform she studied for six years, which involves combining flowers and driftwood in asymmetrical shapes to form living sculpture.

The influence of *ikebana* is obvious in Cebuan's approach to furniture design. She combines unconventional materials, such as sharkskin, burnt coral, melon shells and leather, in airy designs which unnervingly seem to hang together with the fragility of a cobweb – a delicacy more apparent than real. Her surrealist furniture is stronger than it looks!

Cebuan confesses that for her, colour and form are more important than comfort – 'I like to be overtaken by beauty'. But she makes a distinction between 'furniture which I have to use because of necessity' (such as a sofa or desk), where comfort is a major consideration, 'and furniture I am able to scatter around and look at', where it's not.

Light and space are essential qualities of Cebuan's work. She is fascinated by the 'different light that you get during the day, the sun and reflections and shadows on the wall'. The chalky pastels which colour her own Kensington flat – soft peach, aquamarine and old gold – were chosen specifically to maximize the light, and are lavishly combined with inexpensive translucent fabrics to create an opulent atmosphere.

As for space, she 'can't be without it'. Cebuan likes an untrammelled living area which gives out different 'vibrations' according to the time of day. And she needs to be able to change the setting to suit her mood. 'I think it is very difficult to have something which is stable and solid. I have to be able to move things around for a fresh approach.' But however the layout may change, the accent is always on tranquillity. 'It's quite dreamy and in a way, quite theatrical', is how Cebuan sums up her approach.

Cebuan de la Rochette's Design

'When I first saw the plates I was really keen on the idea of creating a 1920s yachting feeling', says Cebuan, 'Next day I crossed it off, because it seemed far too obvious.'

Yet, though there are no overt references to ships in the dining room Cebuan has created for Christine and Roger, the setting contains more than one touch which recalls the seashore. By 'keeping ivory in mind' as the dominant colour, the scheme has a subtle, bleached appearance. And her choice of materials – watered silk pattern wallpaper; seagrass flooring; sharkskin table legs; a flotsam of glass and leather; a gigantic shell, and the *ikebana*-inspired arrangements of willow and bird of paradise flowers, all contribute to this effect.

The influence of *ikebana*, with its emphasis on asymmetrical forms, is especially evident. Hence the narrow, triangular shaped, glass table top, which increases the sense of space in the room. In contrast, the supports beneath are elliptical, modelled on the shape of African beans and covered in natural sharkskin. Tiny drawers are cunningly set into each leg to conceal napkins and cutlery.

Semi-circular glass shelves, which echo the curves of the table supports, now fill the chimney breast recess. This has been extended to provide a tall arched unit, lit from above to highlight the delicate features of the Clarice Cliff dinner service. Again by way of contrast, the alcoves on either side contain shelves of a reverse curve, covered in thick black and tan leather,

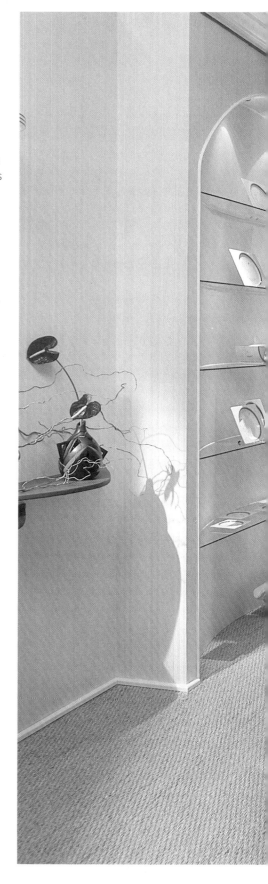

Cebuan's surreal dining room contains furnishings which seem to defy gravity. The glass table top seems to float above its supports and the cobweb chairs, crumpled silk curtains and glass shelves add an air of fragility.

providing a base for *ikebana* flower arrangements.

A similar juxtaposition occurs at the windows, where criss-crossed leather thongs and crumpled silk organza provide an unusual combination. Inner curtains fall straight down over the window to filter the light; whilst outer curtains are knotted together in the centre in a sumptous swag, and carefully crinkled to 'create nice shadows'. Despite appearances this treatment, with the silk at £3 per metre, is far from extravagant.

The thematic contrast between 'delicacy' and 'strength' is at its most evident in Cebuan's chairs, which seem to defy gravity. Made from spun metal, which looks as though it just grew into that shape, they are surprisingly comfortable. The woven canework seats cushion pressure spots and flex with the body, rocking gently with each movement.

Every surface in the room contributes to the overall effect. Even the entrance door is clad in a variegated gold mirror and given a

gilded surround, though generally Cebuan relies on texture rather than pattern or strong colour to convey the mood.

Lighting is especially important in a subtle scheme such as this. Cebuan has used an array of floodlights and downlighters to 'wash' the walls and form pools of light, and provided an elegant candelabra, which echoes the look of the chairs, and without which, she believes, no interior is complete. 'I can't live without candles', she says.

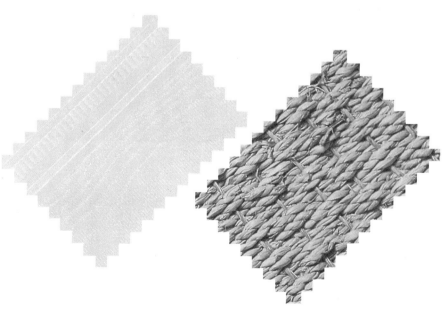

Top left. Curved glass shelves which seem to suspend the china in mid air are balanced by reverse curves covered in leather.

Above and far right. Cebuan's plan sketches, showing the insubstantial dining table and chairs, and the chimney breast transformed into a display unit.

Left. Exotic materials like sharkskin contribute to the light and delicate scheme, and are used to contrast with the rugged seagrass flooring.

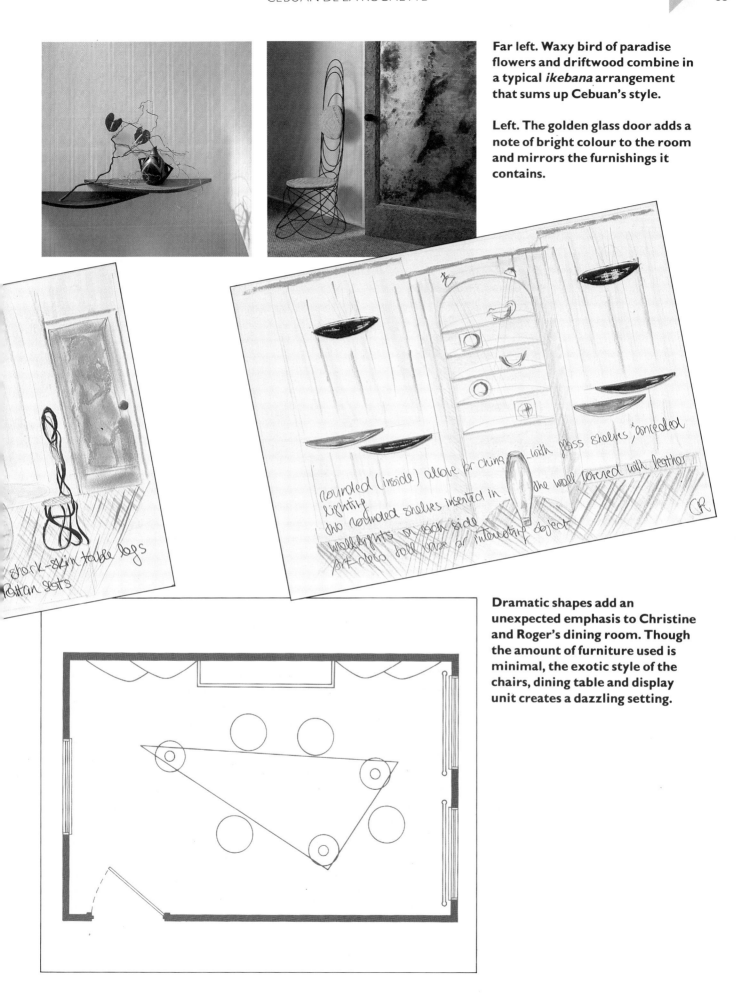

Far left. Waxy bird of paradise flowers and driftwood combine in a typical *ikebana* arrangement that sums up Cebuan's style.

Left. The golden glass door adds a note of bright colour to the room and mirrors the furnishings it contains.

shark-skin table legs
Rattan seats

rounded (inside) alcove for china—with glass shelves, concealed lighting
the rounded shelves inserted in the wall covered with leather
walllights on each side
art-deco doll vase or interesting object

CR

Dramatic shapes add an unexpected emphasis to Christine and Roger's dining room. Though the amount of furniture used is minimal, the exotic style of the chairs, dining table and display unit creates a dazzling setting.

How to Create a Tortoiseshell Finish

The spectacular door that Cebuan de la Rochette created for Roger and Christine's dining room was clad in a special coloured mirror. However, a very similar effect can be achieved using the traditional, and rather less expensive, technique of tortoise-shelling – and it doesn't have to be confined to doors.

Cebuan was working on a simple panelled door, which allowed her to contrast the tortoiseshell effect in the centre panel with a distressed hammered finish on the surround – though sponging (see page 21),

marbling (see page 35) or just a plain coat of paint are equally effective.

If you have plain flush doors, you can pin mouldings to the surface to frame a panel(s), or simply paint a contrasting border on the flat surface – gold, yellows and even deep red provide a suitably opulent contrast to the tortoiseshell.

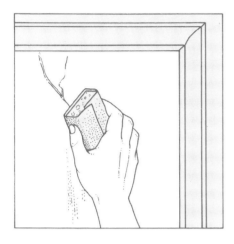

1 On a painted surface, clean with a solution of sugar soap to remove dirt and grease and rinse thoroughly. Fill any cracks, smooth off with sandpaper and key the surface with wet and dry paper. (On bare wood, apply a coat of primer before next stage.)

2 Apply two base coats of an oil-based eggshell paint, in a bright, fairly light, sandy yellow colour, such as chrome. Don't choose too deep or dull a shade, as the following stages will darken the effect considerably.

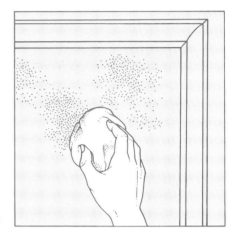

3 Using a brush, apply a fine glaze made from 20% white spirit, 70% scumble and 10% raw sienna artist's oil (all available from artists' suppliers) to the entire surface. Dab the glaze with a lint-free cloth to create a random mottled effect.

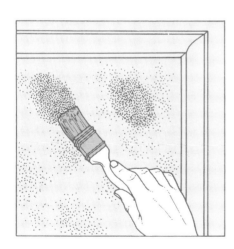

4 Darken glaze with more raw sienna, and apply diagonally in oval shaped patches – use the picture of Cebuan's door for reference. Further darken the glaze with burnt umber (artists' oil), and dab it on with a small brush as smaller marks inside the oval patches.

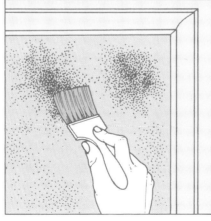

5 Before the above stages dry, add more burnt umber and some black to your glaze and dab small blotches into the centre of the patches created in step 4. Immediately, use a badger brush to soften the edges of the patches, and blur the entire surface.

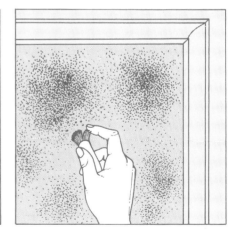

6 Using a stencil brush, spatter a very fine spray of your darkest glaze over the surface – to produce tiny, almost black spots. Allow to dry, and protect the finish with one of two coats of clear matt or silk polyurethane varnish.

The Designer

2   Colin Gold

As a designer who has made his name creating interiors for restaurants, and who numbers a worldwide Japanese-American restaurant chain among his clients, Colin Gold is well qualified to decorate Christine and Roger's dining room. Moreover, he likes to cook and loves to eat – and to extract incautious confessions from his dinner guests.

'The dining room is the only place in the house where innocent guests reveal all over a scrumptious meal', he says.

The large dining area of his own home, a converted school hall near Hackney marshes in London, reflects his belief that the surroundings should draw the eye towards the table. 'Concentration is inwards, not outwards', he says. Apart from a round dining table, draped with a sheet in neo-classical style, and dining chairs, the only furnishings are a chaise longue; a whatnot laden with fruit and pulled up to the table; an oil painting propped against a wall, and a number of urns stacked in the corners. The walls are pale and plain, apart from 'distressed' frescoes of Minoan vases; and the floor is covered by plain wooden board.

As a self-confessed member of café society Colin explains, 'I enjoy eating, I enjoy going out to eat, I enjoy watching other people eat and I enjoy listening to other people talk'. He has reached the conclusion that food and company are all-important, and that hosts bear the responsibility for both. 'They're the ringmasters of the evening', he declares. 'They're not really there for their own entertainment, they've got to make their guests feel at home.'

For Colin, dining is a performance art – so even food must be selected for looks as much as taste. 'You don't just eat with your mouth, but your eyes and ears too', he says. 'It's a multi-sensory experience.'

Colin's design recalls a dining room on an ocean liner, containing rattan chairs, a boat-shaped table and deck-like floorboards.

Colin Gold's Design

'I put together a collection of images that I think are in the client's mind and then I explain what I'm trying to achieve', says Colin Gold, referring to the 'concept boards' he uses to present sketches of his ideas to the client.

On this occasion, the ideas were all maritime because Colin has based his scheme on the Cruiseware china Christine and Roger were anxious to include. Colin feels this theme is particularly appropriate for a dining room because 'on a cruise, dining takes up a major part of the day. It's an important event and I want to recreate that sense of occasion.'

The result is there's scarcely an item in the entire room which would look out of place on an ocean liner, yet it all looks equally appropriate in Christine and Roger's landlocked dining room. Colin has captured the 'essence of promenading' with floorboards defined by a mahogany red border and bleached and scrubbed to give a weathered 'deck' effect; rattan chairs; and a boat-shaped dining table made from cardboard carpet tubes covered with dowelling and MDF (medium density fibreboard) and sprayed a deep lacquer red. Lit by an impressive brass billiard lamp which hangs low over its surface, the table becomes the centrepiece of the room.

Colin kept family diners in mind when creating the table: 'its shape dictates the placing of the diners', he declares, which is why the chairs are ranged in threes down each side – an eminently practical arrangement because the ends can be kept clear for serving. Moreover, 'if the lacquer finish gets scratched you can spray it again', he says, and when the children leave home it could be replaced by one made from a 'glorious wood' like walnut, which would make a splendid addition to the setting.

The room includes many other nautical notions, notably the brass ladders which provide an ingenious and flexible method of displaying pictures, and the sliding storage cabinet Colin has devised for the Clarice Cliff china. The cabinet, based on a ship's locker, has a corniced sliding exterior painted to blend with the walls and imitate the chimney breast opposite, and a mirrored and illuminated interior to enhance the detailed drawings on the Cruiseware.

The cabinet closes when required, to protect the china, but other hatches are less easily battened down. Designed to resemble tarpaulins, the pleated cream curtains are carefully fixed in place for maximum effect. In fact, they are inspired as much by road as water transport, being copied from the Rexine concertina blinds which screen the driver from his passengers in a traditional London bus!

Colin derives his ideas from many sources, and one of these was the decrepit state of the original room: he was delighted with the peeling plaster and has used it as the basis for a stencil. Now the walls are decorated with cream, peach and khaki waves, and a patchy trellis which evokes what interior designer John Fowler once called 'a pleasing decay'. 'It's a distressed finish which looks like the period stencilling you might find on old plaster or old bits of wallpaper', explains Colin.

In marked contrast, he has retained the contemporary style of the fireplace recess. However, the mirrored cabinet opposite, which mimics the chimney breast, moves the focus of the room away from the fireplace to the china. This is in accord with Christine and Roger's wish to keep the service for display rather than dining. 'It's a piece of the history of art', he says, recommending they look at the Cruiseware but lay the table with brass liner plates and plain cream china to reinforce the maritime theme.

Sliding doors conceal and protect the Clarice Cliff Cruiseware when the dining room is not in use but draw apart when required.

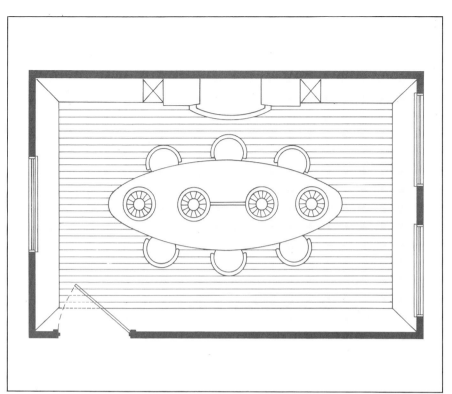

The room is dominated by the great oval table with its six dining chairs ranged each side, to leave the ends free for serving. The display cabinet occupies the wall opposite the chimney breast.

Below left. Though pleated and tied back like tarpaulins, the inspiration for the curtains actually came from the Rexine blinds once seen on every London bus.

Below. Ship's ladders in brass form an original and flexible method of picture display. The distressed wall finish was inspired by the peeling plaster Colin saw on his first visit to Christine and Roger's home!

Below left and right. Colin's initial sketches reveal the importance of the nautical theme, designed to complement the Clarice Cliff china, and the stencilled wall finish which recalls peeling wallpaper.

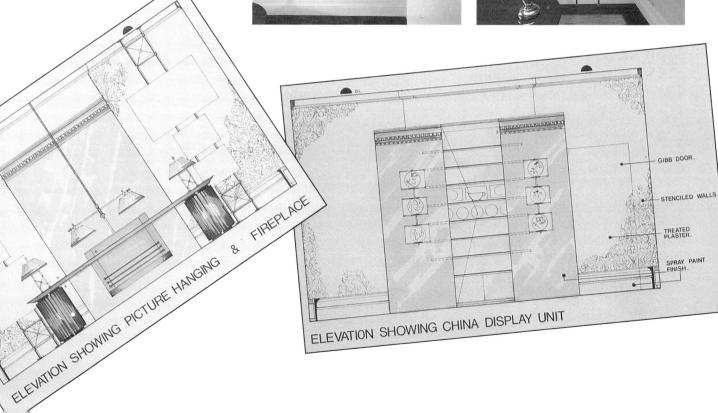

ELEVATION SHOWING PICTURE HANGING & FIREPLACE

ELEVATION SHOWING CHINA DISPLAY UNIT

GIBB DOOR.

STENCILED WALLS.

TREATED PLASTER.

SPRAY PAINT FINISH.

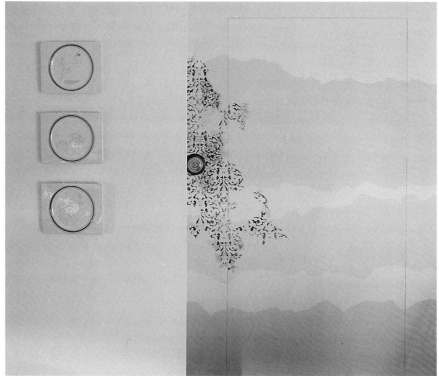

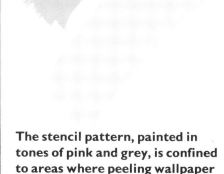

The stencil pattern, painted in tones of pink and grey, is confined to areas where peeling wallpaper might be left clinging to the skirting or an alcove.

How to Create a Peeling Wallpaper Effect

Inspired by the stripped plaster and damaged wallpaper on the fireplace wall in Christine and Roger's original dining room, Colin Gold deliberately recreated this patchy effect to produce another example of a 'distressed finish'.

He washed the walls with bands of different colours and in places stencilled on top a motif taken from a traditional wallpaper design. The effect is as if a paper decorated with soft washes of colour had peeled back to reveal an older and more striking paper underneath.

You will find that this is a simple

technique, but its effectiveness does depend on knowing when to stop. For example, Colin painted some of the walls in plain ivory, rather than with coloured bands, and he restricted the stencilled effect to areas where you would expect old wallpaper to peel. Rub wire wool over for an added burnish and 'ageing' feel.

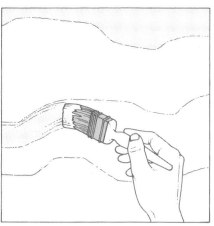

1 Clean dirt and grease from the walls. Fill any cracks and sand smooth. Previously painted surfaces should be keyed by rubbing down with wet and dry paper.

2 Mark the outlines of the bands of colour, using chalk – try to avoid making them too uniform. Mix up three batches of glaze in pink, ivory and grey, using 70% scumble, 20% eggshell paint and 10% white spirit. Brush the glazes into the bands and allow to dry.

3 Copy a small, busy and geometric pattern from a piece of old wallpaper and make up your own stencil (for how to cut and apply a stencil, see page 34). Stencil the motif onto the walls with lilac/grey eggshell paint – using Colin's design for reference.

How to Create a 'Weathered' Deck Effect

The maritime theme Colin Gold introduced to complement the Clarice Cliff china in Roger and Christine's dining room was extended to the floor, which was bleached to resemble the deck of a ship. Colin added a contrasting mahogany red surround to echo the colour of the majestic dining table.

This is a relatively simple effect to reproduce, provided your floorboards are in reasonable condition. Previously stained or varnished boards will need to be prepared with a power sander, which is easy to use and readily available from tool hire shops – but you must wear a dust mask.

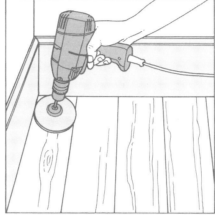

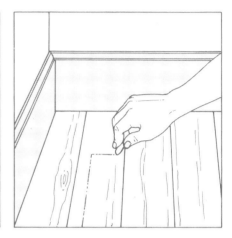

1 Punch nail heads well below surface. Sand boards with powersander, working diagonally across room. At end of sweep, turn around and sand a parallel sweep, overlapping previous one. When finished, sand to opposite diagonal. Use a drum sander for large rooms.

2 Fit medium grade sandpaper to machine and sand along direction of boards. Follow up with fine grade paper to produce smooth finish. (Use an orbital sander or sanding block, for sanding edges by skirting board and awkward corners.)

3 Having vacuumed up all dust, mark out a border around perimeter of room, using a piece of chalk. The width of border will be determined by size of the room – though 30 cm (12 inches) is usually appropriate.

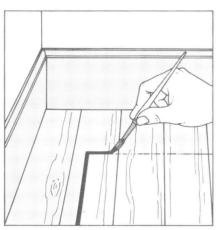

4 Scrub centre boards with wood bleach, rubbing it in direction of grain. When dry, rub in whiting (available from specialist decorator's shops), or apply lime wax, to produce a scrubbed weathered deck effect.

5 Stain border area mahogany red (though there's nothing to stop you using any colour), using a water-based, acrylic or resin-based stain. When dry, paint a 10mm ($\frac{3}{8}$ inch) line in matt black oil-based paint between stained and bleached areas to highlight the contrast.

6 When dry, seal floor with a minimum of three coats of matt finish polyurethane varnish. (A dash of white gloss paint added to the varnish helps to prevent yellowing.)

The Designer

3   Mick Hurd

As a practised and skilful artist, Mick Hurd is less interested in furnishing a room than in re-creating it; treating it as a giant canvas on which to convey exuberant ideas inspired by Michaelangelo, Matisse, Dufy and Mickey Mouse – to name but a few.

Moving from room to room through his own large home in Islington is rather like passing through a series of film sets – not surprising, since Mick studied theatre design at Central School of Art and subsequently worked as a designer in rep. (More recently, he has been assistant art director on a pop video for Boy George and Mel and Kim.)

The stairways in his home are impeccably painted with classical garlands adorning the dado and ceiling; the hall is lined with a parade of papier-mâché antlers worthy of an ancestral home – though their noses are glaring red bulbs which light the way and cock a snook at conventional objets d'art. The study is based on a combination of Matisse's *The Lute* and a Mexican garden, where papier-mâché Mayan figures and primitive masks decorate the walls and, the bathroom, inspired by Dufy's *Kingdom by the Sea*, is painted in blue, white and red, and hung about with giant shells and starfish. The bedroom is a 'Roman temple' splendidly decorated with wreaths, garlands and noble profiles on Etruscan red panels, which are set between a classical frieze and a dado of trompe l'oeil 'drapery'. His living room is a monument to bad taste. 'Anything really nasty can go in there', says Mick, who has built up an unrivalled collection of kitsch, including a print of the Last Supper framed in leopard skin.

The large number of rooms means that 'it doesn't matter if they're a bit wacky or whatever – you can always move to another one', explains Mick. Not quite what Christine and Roger had in mind perhaps, though they did ask to be amazed – and who is more qualified to do that than Mick Hurd?

Kingston, Surrey or Kingston, Jamaica? Mick Hurd exercises his talents as a theatre designer to decorate the dining room as a coral island, complete with lagoon, lobsters and pygmy cannibals.

Mick Hurd's Design

Unlike the two other designers, Mick Hurd was 'unexcited' by the Clarice Cliff dinner service. But it stirred his imagination sufficiently to inspire a scheme which has transformed Christine and Roger's suburban dining room into a Pacific paradise. Hot, tropical colours like cobalt blue, lilac, sand and coral are used throughout the room, which now resembles an island set in a blue lagoon.

Mick says the whole scheme is intended to give the guests 'something to laugh about before the food comes in'. Thus, pygmy cannibals support the elaborate multi-coloured dresser Mick has designed for the china, though obviously they have made contact with western civilization because one of them sports a watch. 'They are smiling', he points out, 'so they're quite friendly really'. At least they have discarded their shields and spears, for these now decorate the upper doors of the display cabinet where

they form a novel coat of arms.

Everything in the room represents something the Cruiseware flappers might have encountered on their way round the world. Hence the deep blue floor and ceiling which represent the sea and sky; the lilac of tropical shadows; the 'seaweed curtains'; the friezes of lobsters, dolphins and shells, and the heaps of sand, 'nets' and 'rope' on the cabinet. Surveying it all is the figure of Neptune who is depicted alone, resting on the globe which serves as his shield, or reclining with a mermaid to form an extravagant pediment on the cabinet. The shield reappears on the ceiling, rising from a sea of leaping fish, while the globe decorates the doors of the cabinet, which is lit from within by a greenish watery light, and adorned with brass handles in the shape of galleons. Even the table, swathed in yards of white fabric, might be a ship in full sail.

Mick was not so much concerned with accuracy when creating some of these features, as to give them a sense

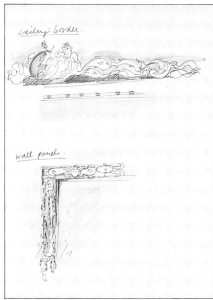

Above. Mick's original designs convey only a little of the exotic decoration eventually to transform the dining room.

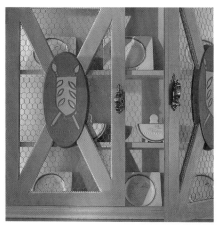

Above. The display cabinet doors are covered with chicken wire to recall fishing nets and are decorated with a coat of arms.

Right. The dark blue ceiling is decorated with leaping fish. At £12,000 the gilt and cobalt chandelier is an optional extra!

of caricature, as in a cartoon. What counts is the overall effect and sheer scale of the scheme, so the odd mistake – or six-legged octopus – is insignificant. Yet despite this 'relaxed' approach, the decorating process can be a long one. ('Some of the rooms in my own house have taken me four months to paint!' admits Mick.) But because little skill is needed 'even an amateur can succeed'. For example, the figures of Neptune and the pygmies are made from papier-mâché. 'Start when you're about five by watching Blue Peter', encourages Mick, who says that with the addition of colour and individual features, the figures 'take on a life of their own'.

Although it looks fantastic, this scheme relies chiefly on paint and costs little more than time – if one ignores the (optional) gilded chandelier at a cool £12,000. The curtains are painted canvas, the dining table was a junk shop find and the display cabinet is made from a combination of softwood, chicken wire and papier-mâché. Even the black dining chairs and the classic marble mantelpiece, with its discreet shell motif, were reasonably priced.

'I wanted to do something extraordinary but I didn't want to mess with the proportions of the room', says Mick, describing his decorative approach. He expects that guests will be 'gobstruck' when they see the result. 'They cannot fail to be amazed when they walk into the room', he says, recommending that Christine and Roger should serve exotic dishes to complement the scheme.

Seafood borders create a visual feast and add interest to plain walls painted in hot tropical shades of sand and coral. The marble mantelpiece makes a restrained contrast – but even that is decorated with a shell motif.

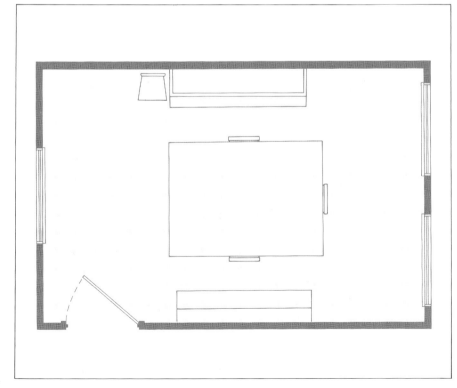

Paint, not furniture, is used to distinguish Mick Hurd's design. As the plan shows, the room contains only a table and chairs, plus a wall cupboard which contains the Cruiseware china.

How to Paint Decorative Panels and Friezes

When Mick Hurd painted the friezes and panels which decorate Christine and Roger's dining room, he was less concerned with the accuracy of the lobsters, dolphins, shells, nets and rope than with giving them a sense of cartoon-like caricature.

If you wish to reproduce such features you don't have to be an accomplished fine artist. They can be fairly crude – the odd mistake here and there won't matter, as it's the overall effect that counts.

The technique outlined below will enable you to copy and transfer the basic shapes of figures and motifs from books and magazines onto the surfaces of your room. Using templates is a particulary efficient method of reproducing a large number of repeating motifs – as in Mick's dolphin frieze. To finish off, all you have to do is colour them in freehand.

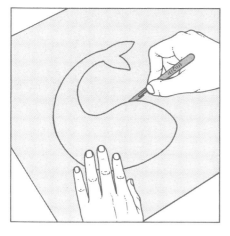

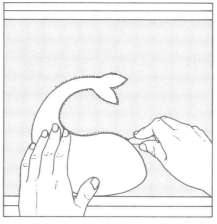

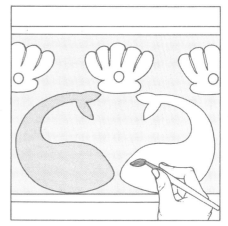

1 Place sheet of tracing paper over picture of figure or motif to be copied, and trace outline. Transfer this onto piece of card, and cut out shape (in this case a dolphin) to make a template. Motifs can be enlarged on photocopier (see page 99).

2 Prepare surface for paint, using spirit level and chalk to mark outlines of panel or frieze, and low-tack masking tape to shield sides. Apply template and trace outline with chalk, repeating as necessary. Fill in background colour with two coats of emulsion.

3 When background paint is dry, paint in details (using Mick's dolphins for reference). When dry, define outline of motif with contrasting colour for a cartoon-like effect and paint over with glaze. Remove masking tape along edge of frieze.

Christine and Roger's Conclusion

Christine was amazed by Mick Hurd's design. 'It reminds me of an Indian dress fabric or a maharajah's palace, all glittery and sparkly.' But not the sort of room she could see herself walking into every day, and Roger doubted the pygmies would last long with the children around.

'I found Cebuan's scheme attractive because it was light and spacious', said Roger, although he objected to the 'clash of materials' and insisted that 'the table legs remind me of rugby balls, and I don't want rugby balls holding up the dinner table'. Christine disliked the glass table top, 'because you can see everyone's feet underneath', but approved of Cebuan's drapes.

In contrast, they found Colin Gold's scheme practical as well as stylish – liking the colours, the table and chairs and, especially, the display cabinet for their china. 'It's great, I could live with that', said Christine.

THE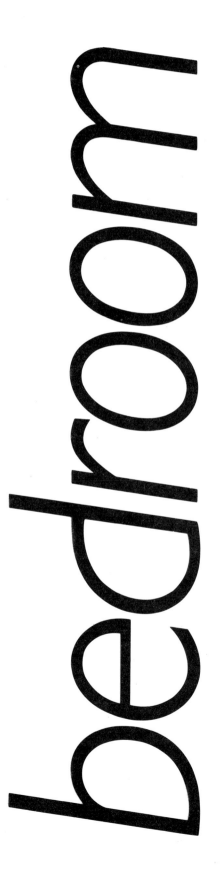

bedroom

Somewhere to sleep, somewhere to retreat, somewhere to unwind – whatever you are doing bedrooms are for the most part private and intimate areas which allow you to indulge your decorative fantasies. If, like our couple Pat and Alec Lewis, you are lucky enough to have a large, sunny room to furnish as your bedroom, it seems a waste to use it simply as a place to sleep. Most people, especially the parents of young children, find that the bedroom is the only place to escape from the demands of the family – most of the time! You can use this freedom to indulge in the pale colours and delicate finishes that can't be risked in the rest of the house, and you can allow the room to become a place where arrangements of china or precious objects can be displayed in relative safety.

True, if you want to create such a sanctum there are practical considerations as well. Storage space is essential, for in addition to clothing you may need to store seasonal necessities like suitcases, sportswear or extra bedding in the room. Would fitted or free-standing wardrobes be more appropriate? Would you prefer a sofa or an easy chair for quiet pursuits like reading and embroidery, and can they be accommodated in the available space? Certainly you would want a dressing table or a chest with a mirror, but where is the best position for it in the room? Most of us appreciate something underfoot to soften the impact of rising from bed, but your budget may not run to a fitted carpet – if not, what are the alternatives, and how do they look with the rest of the decor? How can you allow a large window to admit plenty of light when it is also necessary to screen it from the house opposite, or from a passing bus? It can be difficult to reconcile these different objectives and still create the room of your dreams – have a look at the solutions proposed by our experts.

THE ORIGINAL BEDROOM

Alec and Pat Lewis are an artistic couple who hail from the Welsh valleys. Alec is an advertising agency art director, and Pat an expert needlewoman. They have an active toddler and, like thousands of other couples, a Victorian terraced house which they are in the process of restoring.

'I hate the wallpaper; it doesn't do anything for the panelling, and I think the room could be far more elegant.' This was Pat Lewis's verdict on the decor she and her husband Alec woke up to every morning.

In its place they wanted a traditional style – more in keeping with the Victorian cast iron fireplace, complete with gold and turquoise tiles, they had uncovered while restoring the house.

Though they were delighted to find the fireplace still intact, they were not sure how to incorporate its strong colours into a decorative scheme which they both agreed must be light and restful.

The existing decor was dominated by 70s style browns: the mantelpiece was painted brown, the carpet was patterned with great swirls of brown, and the cream coloured walls were embellished with mouldings (brown, of course), which formed panels around a dated, mini-print wallpaper with a brown motif.

Into this setting Pat and Alec had introduced an Edwardian dressing table and a vast free-standing wardrobe. For sentimental reasons they wanted to retain these pieces in the new scheme, though they agreed they could be painted, if necessary. They also wanted to retain the double bed, and the round table where Pat sits to sew, and which they use for Sunday breakfast in bed. However, they were unsure what the designers would make, if anything, of their collection of mannequin heads, erotic art and a tailor's dummy!

Fixtures they did not want to change

included the fireplace and the mouldings which formed the panels on the walls. The latter, unlike the cornice and picture rail, were not original. They had been put up by the previous owner of the house, but the Lewises believed that they helped to emphasise the graceful proportions of the room.

As to their priorities: Alec was concerned with privacy, because the houses opposite were so close. Pat had toyed with the idea of hanging tiered curtains at the window, so that the bottom layer could be closed while the top was drawn to admit light. But on this, as on most other points, the Lewises were happy to leave the final decision to the designers – though they did point out that whatever the scheme, it would have to withstand occasional dawn raids from a very small boy and a very large dog.

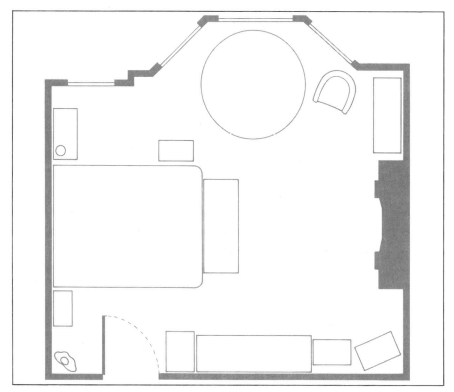

WITH ITS LARGE BAY WINDOW AND REDISCOVERED VICTORIAN FIREPLACE THIS IS POTENTIALLY A PLEASANT ROOM. ITS SIZE MAKES IT EASY TO FURNISH AND THOUGH THE OFFSET BAY CREATES AN ASYMMETRICAL EFFECT, THE EXTRA WINDOW ADDS TO THE LIGHT AND AIRY EFFECT.

BROWN PAINT, BEIGE AND CREAM
WALLPAPER AND SWIRLING CARPET
MAKE THE ROOM LOOK BOTH DULL
AND DATED.

FOUR WINDOWS FLOOD THE ROOM
WITH LIGHT BUT AS THE HOUSE IS CLOSE
TO THE ROAD, PRIVACY CAN BE
QUITE A PROBLEM.

THE WALL PANELS ARE A RELATIVELY
NEW ADDITION BUT HELP TO IMPROVE
THE PROPORTIONS OF THE ROOM BY
BALANCING THE HIGH CEILING.

The Designer

1 Stephen Calloway

Well known museum curator and writer and authority on taste, Stephen Calloway not only works at the Victoria and Albert Museum in London, but dresses in period – complete with frock coat, waistcoat and cravat, beard and waxed moustache and *pince-nez*. His passion for the past naturally extends to furnishings, and he is fortunate that his base at the V & A gives him access to an unparalleled resource of information about past decorative arts. Indeed, at the moment he is working on a book on interior design.

However, his approach is far from purist. He likes to play with historical styles to bring them into the twentieth century – though the 1830s is his 'absolutely favourite era'. He sums up his philosophy as an attempt 'to combine the very best of the new and the best of the old, so that the old informs the new and the new becomes something exciting'.

Mixing styles successfully is possible, Stephen believes, because the principles which underlie good design are constant. Not that he takes them too seriously. He tends to imitate the sense of fun which inspired the eighteenth century's follies, gazebos and trompe l'oeil designs. 'I always try to include some element of surprise or fantasy in every room', he says.

At the V & A Stephen has emphasised the grandeur of The Painted Room (the director's dining room), by rendering it devoid of furniture to reveal its perfect proportions. In this homage to the spirit of architecture, the wall panels, surmounted by bows, are each painted in a specific style – Gothic, Palladian and so on. And he has used a number of stone coloured fantasy paint finishes, from a fossilised effect on the mantelpiece to 'rusticated' trompe l'oeil stonework beneath the dado, to complement the grey-blue, soft pink and gold panelling. An oversize copy of an eighteenth-century chandelier and a baroque style mirror, made by a contemporary ceramicist, complete the picture.

Not surprisingly, Stephen holds strong views about colour. Bedrooms, for example, should either be dark and powerful or pale and virtually colourless. He spurns the middle way, and cannot tolerate safe 'porridge' colours, which are totally at variance with his belief that 'a room without surprises is a dull room'.

Bedroom into boudoir: Stephen Calloway uses swags of spotted net to create this sumptuous and romantic setting.

Stephen Calloway's Design

'Marie Antoinette meets Joan Collins', might sum up the transformation of the Lewises' suburban bedroom into a romantic haven.

In fact, the room is decorated in Gone with the Wind ante-bellum style – though in contrast to Scarlett O'Hara, who wore her curtains, Stephen draped yards of voile over almost every piece of freestanding furniture (see 'how to drape fabric', page 72). Structural items, such as windows, doors and the mantelpiece are all swathed in spotted net, and even the pictures are equipped with modesty veils to conceal the 'bedroom art'. However, the fabrics are relatively cheap, and thus can be used lavishly.

The effect is ethereal, because every material is chosen to filter the light; even the ladder-like chairs have an insubstantial appearance.

'The idea is to bring a sense of grandeur and symmetry to a type of room which normally lacks these

qualities', Stephen explains. The panelling was 'poorly proportioned', and so goes. The 'ugly picture rail' is removed, to increase the visual height of the room. The equally ill-thought-of chimney piece is marbled, to match the wardrobe and entrance door, and the fireplace tiles are obliterated with white paint – to blend in with the misty coloured scheme, and because they are 'too hideous to keep' in their original colours. 'It's best not to be too reverent about Victorian speculative builders' tastes', says Stephen.

What has been added is a miniature conservatory, consisting of a false partition and a pair of doors which give access to the original window. The inside of it has been fitted out to display plants – so the Lewises will wake up to sunlight filtering through the greenery.

This memorable feature has an architectural purpose: it is designed to improve the symmetry of the window bay, and has the additional advantage of removing the need for heavy curtains to preserve privacy. Instead,

the new windows are dressed with white spotted voile, ruched and secured with ribbon rosettes to form a swagged pelmet.

To increase the sense of space, mirrored panels are fixed beside each conservatory door. They reflect 'round' tables, which are in fact semi-circular – a piece of visual trickery that's typical of the Calloway style. Like the dressing and bedside tables they are draped with grey glazed chintz, which also hangs from a corona above the bed.

That's not all: a chandelier replaces the original pendant light; a star lantern illuminates the conservatory and there's even a servants' bell beside the fireplace – alas, purely for show.

By contrast, other features and surfaces are quite plain: the walls are painted in grey and white stripes; the floorboards are simply stripped, stained and polished, and home comforts are provided in the shape of rugs cut from carpet and bound with black edging to emphasise the monochrome scheme – one of the few dark touches in this pale and translucent room.

Below right. Stephen Calloway's design features a bijou conservatory whose inner windows are draped with lengths of voile.

Below left. Translucent spotted net is draped over grey-blue sheen, and set off with toning smoky blue fringing.

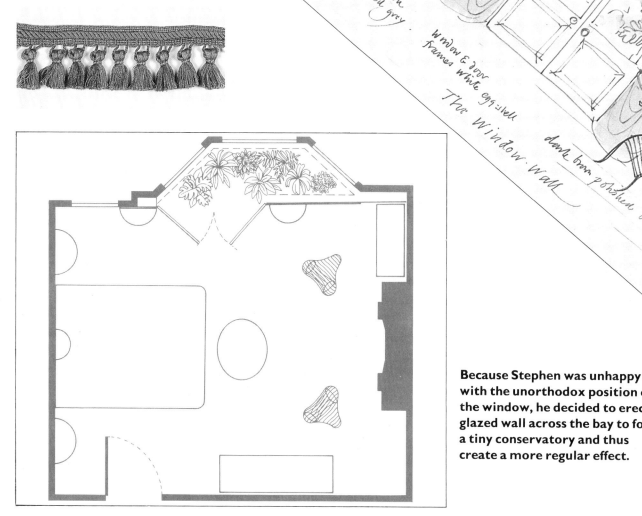

Because Stephen was unhappy with the unorthodox position of the window, he decided to erect a glazed wall across the bay to form a tiny conservatory and thus create a more regular effect.

Right. The impressive corona or baldachino which surmounts the bed is made from a pair of curtains hung from a semi-circle of plywood and draped behind hold-backs to reveal the lining.

bows and gathered balls of fabric.

Walls painted in wide white & grey stripes slightly irregular

Right. Every fixture from the dresser to the door is swathed in spotted net in the appropriate Victorian manner.

broomstick brass arrow ends and brackets.

Door grained with black mouldings

paint rimlock black. Get brass knob

Dismissive of 'Victorian speculative builders' tastes', Stephen has obliterated the colours of the fireplace tiles.

How to Drape Fabric

It is important to be lavish with fabric if you wish to create a dramatic effect, but you must choose something lightweight that will drape well, such as voile or net, and avoid slippery or bulky materials. Stephen Calloway suggests the addition of bows or rosettes, or tie-backs and plaits, for an attractive finishing touch.

I Take a length of fabric and use a staple gun or tacks to secure it to one end of the batten, pole, or window frame. Alternatively, simply twist and knot it to secure in position.

2 Ruching the fabric allows it to drape into a deep swag. Secure it in place one-sixth of the way along the pole or frame, repeating until you reach the far end.

3 Allow sufficient fabric to fall down at each end to form tails – adding tie-backs or bows if required. Finish by covering knots, staples or tacks with ribbon rosettes.

How to Make a Corona

As Stephen has done in the Lewises' room, make an elaborate baldachino, or corona, to create a sumptuous fairytale bed. More practical than a four poster in the average bedroom, it gives an air of importance to the simplest divan, costs relatively little and does not interfere with bedmaking or obscure the light.

It is a good idea to use a medium-weight material for the back curtain and a sheer, lightweight fabric for the side drapes. This will prevent the corona appearing heavy or cumbersome, and allow you to choose more than one of the fabrics used elsewhere in the room. For an elegant finishing touch secure the curtains to brass or painted wooden hold-backs at each side of the bed, using ribbon bows or heavy cord.

1 Mark out and cut a semi-circle of 12 mm ($\frac{1}{2}$ in) plyboard or chipboard to the diameter required (this will vary depending on the size of bed the corona is intended for).

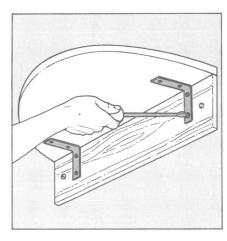

2 Screw a wooden batten securely to the wall (taking care to locate the joists if it is a stud wall) at the required height. Fix the semi-circular board securely in place, using angle brackets.

3 Turn top, bottom and side hems on the back curtain, and run two rows of gathering threads along the top edge. Pull in the fabric to the correct width, and tack or staple the top of the curtain just below the semi-circular board, to hide the angle brackets.

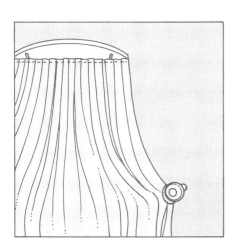

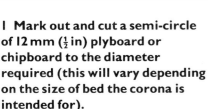

4 Screw the hold-back hooks or knobs in position on the wall, in line with the edges of the bed. Sew braid loops to the outer hems of the back curtain, and hook them over the hold-backs. As a result, the curtain will fan out to form the back of the corona.

5 Turn the top, bottom and side hems of the two side curtains, adding a frill or fringe if required. Sew in two rows of gathering threads, and pull in the fabric. Tack or staple the curtains to the top of the corona. Then, hang the drapes over the hold-backs.

6 Tack a braided fringe and bow around the head of the corona and finally, use an offcut of fabric from the back curtain to cover the underneath of the semi-circular frame, and sew on braid or fringing to conceal the staples or tacks.

The Designer

2 Cressida Bell

Great-niece of novelist Virginia Woolf and granddaughter of painter Vanessa Bell, Cressida Bell finds the family tree an encumbrance at times – which is why she chose first fashion and then textile design as the outlet for her own artistic talents. 'It was something no one in the family had done before', she explains.

Cressida has had considerable success, particularly with furnishing fabrics, and her printed scarves sell widely under her own label in many shops. Moreover, designing fabrics for Liberty and Warners has given her access to a world-wide market – Bloomsbury meets Bloomingdales!

Working from a studio in Hackney, Cressida concentrates on printed scarves, though she has created designs for wallpaper and tiles, and is a dab hand with paint techniques. All her fabrics are screen printed by hand, and are decorated with simple trompe l'oeil motifs such as scrolls and Celtic wheels, or basic geometrics, like circles bisected by diagonal lines or set into squares.

Much of her inspiration comes from ethnic, especially Turkish art. However, there is an undeniable Bloomsbury air about her work and the way in which she uses it. Like Vanessa Bell she employs a lot of pattern to produce an effect that is both bold and pretty. 'My work is less obviously Bloomsbury than it was a few years ago, but once you think about it you can still see the influence', she says. 'You either embrace it or reject it, but it's still there.'

Decorated in blue and gold to complement the fireplace, the room has a distinct 20s flavour.

Cressida Bell's Design

Working with three dimensions rather than two was a novelty for Cressida. She had not designed an interior before, though obviously was very familiar with soft furnishings like curtains, cushions and bedspreads.

In keeping with her enthusiasm for decorative paint techniques (her first bedroom was sponge stencilled, she remembers), the mantelpiece, dressing table and wardrobe are painted in a 3-D geometric pattern using nothing more than eggshell, a set square and imagination (see 'how to give a fire surround a trompe l'oeil finish', page 79). The design is inspired by the carving on the mantelpiece, but in contrast to the sharp lines of the pattern, the colours used are soft blues, greys, creams and yellows. They help to mute the effect of the bright, fireplace tiles.

Yellow features again on the walls, offset by the panelling and picture rail which are painted a greyish-blue. A simple but effective pattern embellishes the inside of the panels, and is created with just a stencil brush and a dinner plate (see 'how to stencil circle motifs', page 78). Confining paint treatments to small areas like this makes light work of decorating, explains Cressida, and also helps to personalize the room without stretching the budget.

Visual interest is strengthened by the use of Cressida's patterned fabrics at the window, as a bedspread, for cushions and as a throw to cover the blanket box at the foot of the bed.

A traditional, loose covered easy chair is introduced, and the Lewises' old

Lloyd loom chair is salvaged with a coat of white paint and filled with cushions. Storage space for books and ornaments is provided by shelving painted in the room's dominant colour – soft blue. Even the lampshades are integrated into the scheme, being embellished with a motif to match the one on the panelled walls.

A personal touch is the simple treatment of the bed, for Cressida cannot bear 'anything over her head'. She freely admits to designing the sort of room she would like to have –

where 'you can sit on the bed and everything is around you. Everything good is within view, rather than behind you'.

However, in other respects the room is planned to suit the Lewises' requirements. The round table is in its usual place in front of the bay window, which is screened from the road, as requested, by translucent, pleated blinds. Even the Lewises' mannequin heads and tailor's dummy, now draped with scarves and a fox fur, are incorporated in the new scheme.

Moreover, the room is decorated to a tight budget – the only extravagances being the blue carpet, the copious fabrics and a piece of sculpture by Cressida's father, Quentin Bell.

It's a cosy room, with an undeniably twentieth century quality about it. But a room that cannot be assigned to any particular decade or style – unless it's that of the Bloomsbury Set.

Above left. The simple window treatment combines full pleated curtains over a translucent screen.

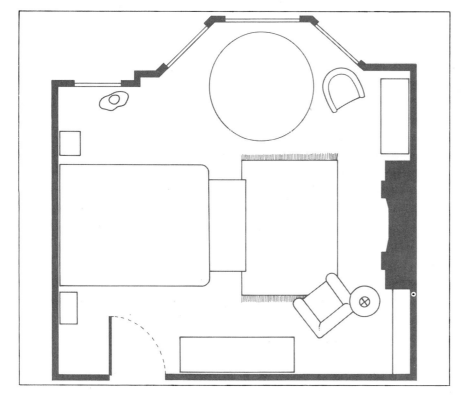

To make this as much a living room as a bedroom, Cressida has provided bookshelves in the alcoves by the chimney breast and added an armchair to complement the existing round table.

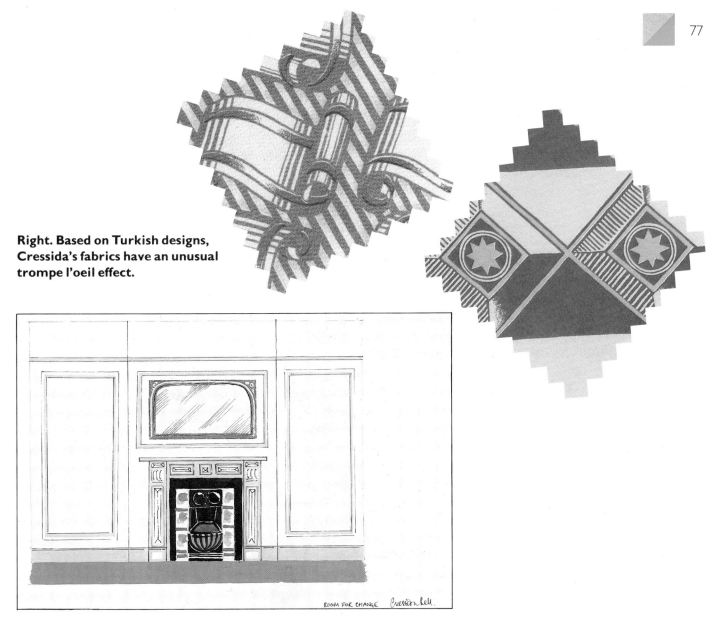

Right. Based on Turkish designs, Cressida's fabrics have an unusual trompe l'oeil effect.

ROOM FOR CHANGE Cressida Bell.

Above. Cressida's sketch of her fireplace treatment shows a 3-D effect uniting the style of the fabrics and the colour of the tiles.

Right. Decorated with soft stencils and outlined in blue, the panels add interest to the walls.

How to Stencil Circle Motifs

The circle motifs that embellish the decorative scheme Cressida Bell has created for the Lewises' bedroom are quick and easy to reproduce.

They can be applied to virtually any surface (you should use fabric paints when working on textiles), and various effects can be produced – depending on the colours used and where the motifs are positioned.

They are best sited within bordered areas, so Cressida has 'framed' them within the wall panels and on the lampshade – contrasting white on yellow with a more strident white on blue.

You might like to experiment with different paint combinations to vary the subtlety of contrast between the motifs and their background. (But try this on spare paper before starting in earnest on the room!)

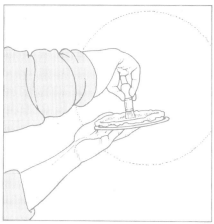

1 Draw around a dinner plate on white card, and cut out to form a template. Place it on the surface you wish to stencil and draw around it with a soft pencil.

2 Using the appropriate paint and a stencil brush, dab a series of rough circles within the outline. Then, rub out the pencil line.

3 Repeat the procedure over the required surface making sure that the circles are positioned evenly within the area.

Right. The fireplace is the focal point of the room, bringing together the colours used in the scheme. The circle motifs on the lampshade echo those painted on the walls.

How to Give a Fire Surround a Trompe l'Oeil Finish

If you have a traditional fire surround you can give it an unusual finish by painting its mouldings to produce a 3-D trompe l'oeil effect. In the Lewises' bedroom Cressida has used darker and lighter tones of colour to emphasize the play of light and shade on the fireplace, and thereby bring out the depth of the mouldings.

This technique is particularly effective for making the most of the sometimes crude features found on early, mass produced fittings. However, the real beauty of it is that it can be used to equal effect on all kinds of surfaces, such as doors, frames, skirtings or fabrics, even if they are featureless or flat.

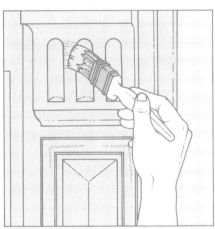

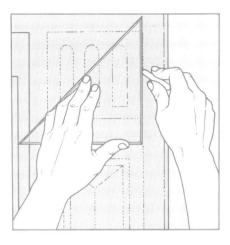

1 Sand down the fire surround to provide a key for the new paintwork. Then clean the surface with white spirit and a rag, and allow to dry.

2 Prime if necessary, and follow with two coats of eggshell over the entire surface, using the colour of your choice (Cressida used mid-blue/grey).

3 This stage is necessary only if you are working on a flat surface; use a soft pencil, a rule and, where necessary, a set-square to simulate the outline of carved mouldings. If you wish, copy Cressida's design.

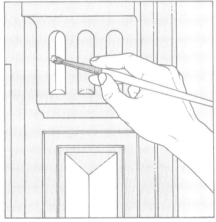

4 Select a colour (Cressida used yellow) and add white to produce two batches of paint – one light, one dark. Apply the paler tone to the sides of each moulding nearest the light. When dry, apply the darker tone to the sides furthest from the light.

5 Take a darker version of the base colour (in this case deep blue/grey) and use it to colour in the areas of deepest shadow inside the mouldings – these tend to be nearest the edge and at the top and bottom.

6 To add definition use the darker version of the base colour to outline a few shapes, such as the triangular base of a raised panel or a simple rectangular border.

The Designer

3 Nicholas Haslam

Society designer Nicholas Haslam, who creates homes for the rich and famous, first showed his flair for interior decoration at Eton – where he hung his room with tiger skin curtains, topped by pelmets of ostrich plume. That gives you an idea of his personal style.

Nicholas's present London flat is equally baroque. His dining room. with its marble table, fine china, gold cutlery and walls resembling beaten metal pierced by silver bars, is a recreation of his favourite room in the palace of the Amalienburg outside Munich. The idea was that 'like a sleeping beauty, the room should look as though it has been abandoned for two hundred years, as though the clock stopped when the mob stormed Versailles'.

His country house is less theatrical, and is decorated principally in classic English country house style. He is well known for this look, with its wallpapers, fresh colours and flowered chintzes; though he does feel it is important to decorate a room in the context and period of the rest of the house.

Much of Nicholas's work is on projects where no expense is spared, and he agrees 'it is very nice – and very rare – to have carte blanche on costs'. However, he is in no doubt that he can create a comfortable, and not too expensive room for Alec and Pat; 'I can't bear anything that is expensive for its own sake', he declares – though he adds that 'the more you spend the nicer the room becomes'.

Traditional furnishings invest the Lewises' suburban bedroom with country house style.

Nicholas Haslam's Design

All rooms should be dual-purpose, thinks Nicholas Haslam, which is why he was delighted to change the Lewises' bedroom into what he describes as 'a very upmarket bedsitter'.

His first impressions of the room were favourable. He liked its basic shape, as well as the cornice and the fireplace, but thought that the bed lacked definition – a deficiency overcome by draping fabric behind the curved bedhead and topping it with a

frilled valance, to recall a traditional tester bed (see 'how to make a frilled valance', page 84).

This treatment helps to bridge the gap between the low furniture and the high ceiling; and the existing mouldings, now painted blue, break up the wall space elsewhere. The effect is reinforced by full length curtains, with a valance like the one above the bed, draped at the window.

Co-ordinated floral fabrics, in shades of cobalt, beige and gold, introduce a feeling of softness as well as adding visual interest. Cool shades of blue are chosen to produce a deceptively haphazard 'bluish effect', which both echoes and tones down the bright turquoise of the fireplace tiles (from which the russet and gold also take their cue).

The room contains at least seven different patterns – on the bed and upholstery, covering the table and sewn into the curtains and cushions – but there is nothing mannered about the way they relate to each other. Nicholas likes to mix as many fabrics as possible, because he believes that the interplay of colour and texture is one of the most important aspects of interior decoration – 'courage is all'. Hence, the woven bedspread, lace-trimmed sheets and cotton prints dressing the bed, and the long, patterned curtains, short sheers and louvre (painted blue, to match the panelling), at the window.

The room is filled with furniture as well as fabric, but careful arrangement, off-white walls and plain carpet give it an air of spacious elegance and prevent

2 yellow + blue above

it appearing overcrowded. It contains everything for the Sunday morning sybarite: from a daybed and a button-backed chair in the window bay, to a butler's tray, a hamper heaped with magazines, an ottoman for the television set and a couple of oval-backed chairs, painted cream, to match the bedside tables.

Tucked into the alcove beside the fireplace, now complete with an easy-to-use gas log fire, is the Lewises' dressing table. The original round table is moved to a more prominent position, and covered with a blue floor length cloth. It now displays a charming arrangement of ornaments and photographs in silver frames.

The Edwardian wardrobe has the luxury of a wall to itself, but otherwise not an inch of space is wasted. Plates supported on brackets decorate the angle between the two windows; there's more china on the mantelpiece, and there are lamps everywhere – by the bed and on the tables. What has vanished is Pat and Alec's collection of erotic art. 'The place for that', says Nicholas firmly, 'is the bathroom'.

Top. Nicholas Haslam's sketch reveals a bedroom to relax in, where comfortable seating is as important as a good night's sleep.

Centre. A blue louvre co-ordinates with curtains at the bay window, which provides an ideal site for the day bed.

Bottom. Traditional chintzes and floral prints are employed to emphasize the blue of the fireplace tiles and to tone down the yellow to rust and brown.

Muted shades of blue and gold form the basis of Nicholas Haslam's colour scheme.

Above. A valanced pelmet and co-ordinating upholstered bedhead give the double divan a sense of grand style.

Above. The size of the room and the position of the bay window allows for a spacious seating area.

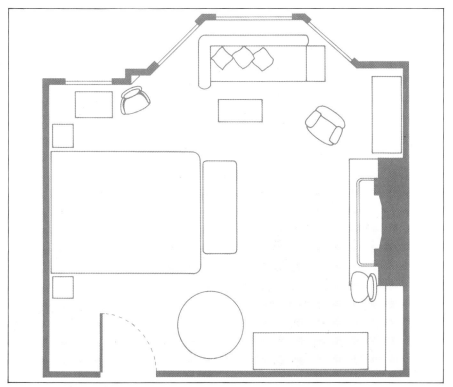

In Nicholas Haslam's design every piece of furniture is carefully placed. The sleeping section contains the bed, side tables and an ottoman which supports a television, while the seating area includes a day bed, fireside and upright chairs plus a low table for snack meals – and he has incorporated Pat and Alec's existing furniture too.

How to Make a Frilled Valance

A valance always provides the perfect finishing touch for formal curtains. It will hide the track or heading and can provide additional height – especially effective in a high-ceilinged room. When used in combination with drapes to simulate a half-tester, as Nicholas Haslam has done in the Lewises' bedroom, it can make an elegant and luxurious addition to even the most ordinary bed.

You must first choose your gathering or pleating tape, as this will dictate the amount of fabric you will need to buy. Pencil pleat and pinch pleat styles are readily available (from the haberdashery departments of most large stores), but you will find box pleats and ornate smocked styles particularly effective for the type of setting that Nicholas has created.

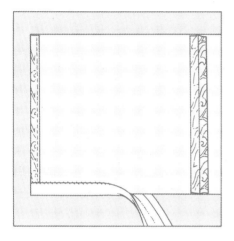

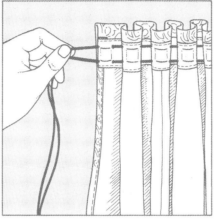

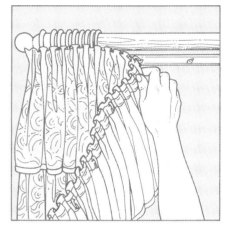

1 Cut the number of fabric widths required, allowing for pattern repeats, seams, headings and hems. Seam together and, if you wish, define the edges with binding which picks up the colour of fabric, such as the bed linen, elsewhere in the room.

2 Sew on the gathering tape according to the manufacturer's instructions, and pull up and space the pleats. To ensure the valance hangs well fix the tape 5cm (2 in) from the top of the fabric, and attach a panel of iron-on inter-lining, to add stiffness and weight.

3 Hang the finished valance from a projecting track (available with fixing instructions from most department stores), clipped to the curtain rail with extension brackets. This will allow the curtains to be drawn without them snagging.

Pat and Alec's Conclusion

Baroque, Bloomsbury or country house? The Lewises chose the last, and Pat was particularly impressed by the way Nicholas Haslam had interpreted their wishes to create a traditional and comfortable room.

Though intrigued by Stephen Calloway's swathes of voile, they decided that their toddler and the dog made his scheme impractical. And as a matter of personal taste, they preferred country house elegance to Bloomsbury charm. 'My favourite is definitely Nicholas Haslam', said Pat – who has yet to count the cost.

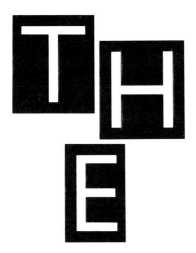

THE CHILD'S ROOM

Children's bedrooms are among the most frequently decorated of all rooms in the home; perhaps because those charming nursery schemes can seem inappropriate in a surprisingly short space of time. (Remember the young teenager Adrian Mole and his Noddy wallpaper?). A cot, small-scale furniture and washable surfaces are needed for only a short period in a child's life – and yet they are indispensable in the first few years. So, the main challenge facing every parent who has to decorate a child's room is how to reconcile short and long term needs – for example, how to provide storage space that will cater initially for toys and later on for compact discs; and how to bring clothes within the reach of a six as well as a sixteen year old.

This is why the three designers chosen for this particular task were asked to design a room to grow with the child. The furnishing had to outlast changes in taste and withstand years of hard wear. Safety and imaginative use of space were to be important considerations and, if possible, the decoration should help bridge the gap between toddler and teenager.

Such requirements are difficult, but not impossible to fulfil. A two year old may look lost in a full size bed, but a pictorial frieze around the walls, a low coat rack in the wardrobe and a favourite teddy will help cut the adult world down to size. A large cupboard can be stacked with toys for now, and later filled as fashion dictates. Even the decor, if chosen with care, can be adapted to keep pace with a child's preferences.

Parents have a particular responsibility in this area, because what they choose can mould as well as reflect a child's taste. The furnishings and decoration provided must be more than practical, safe and comfortable, for they will give children their first experience of colour, form and the decorative arts.

THE ORIGINAL CHILD'S ROOM

Dermott and Tricia George, Scots living in London, organize educational exchanges and tours for musicians. Now redecorating their house, they have firm opinions on colour and design – though their two year old son, Christopher hasn't any strong views, as yet, on how he wants his room done.

'We want a room that will grow with the child.' This summed up Tricia and Dermott George's approach to the room they were planning for their son Christopher – and as he is only two years old both room and boy have a lot of changes ahead.

Christopher was about to make the transition from cot to bed – an event that marks the end of babyhood, so his parents wanted the furnishings to reflect his widening range of interests, and were prepared to invest in quality furniture, providing it was strong enough to last until he was a teenager.

They requested a work surface suitable for games now and homework later on; and a second bed, which would permit friends to stay the night – not easy to provide in a room which, though an adequate size (it measures 2.5 by 3.4 metres/8 by 11 ft), is an awkward shape. There is a large radiator beneath the south-facing sash window, which restricts furniture arrangements, and a chimney breast that projects in front of the door.

Despite this the Georges were reluctant to make structural changes, and not only because of the expense involved. 'We want to retain the basic character of the house', Dermott explained. 'We don't mind spending money on furniture if it will last, but we don't want to waste money taking out the chimney breast.' The radiator was another fixture which had to stay in position – though they were happy to lose the tacky pelmet above the window.

As working parents they took a practical approach to furnishing Christopher's room, requesting duvet covers to simplify bed-making; storage for clothing and toys; a desk lamp to supplement the existing pendant light, and a window blind to shade the sunny room from late afternoon and early morning sun. The selection of wall and floor coverings was left to the individual designer, though both Tricia and Dermott stressed the need to take a toddler's messy lifestyle into account. In particular, they were not convinced that wallpaper was a practical choice.

Their taste ran to strong colours and plain surfaces, though they were willing to experiment with paint treatments such as stencilling, and as Christopher was too young to voice his own opinions they rejected pretty and frilly effects on his behalf.

NO WONDER CHRISTOPHER LOOKS FORLORN. DEVOID OF DECORATION, ALL THE FURNISHINGS THE BEDROOM CONTAINS IS A FIREPLACE AND BUILT-IN CUPBOARD.

CHRISTOPHER'S ROOM HAS SEVERAL
AWKWARD FEATURES, WHICH RESTRICT
THE SCOPE OF THE DESIGNS. A LARGE
RADIATOR IS SET IMMEDIATELY BENEATH
THE WINDOW ON ONE WALL, WHILE
THE ADJACENT WALL IS OCCUPIED BY
THE FIREPLACE, A BUILT-IN CUPBOARD
AND THE ENTRANCE DOOR.

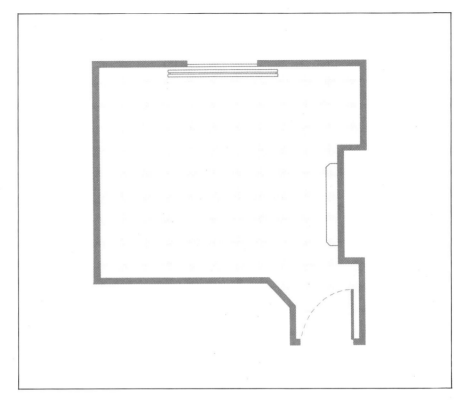

THE SHAPE OF THE ROOM MAKES IT
DIFFICULT TO CHOOSE A FURNITURE
ARRANGEMENT WHICH ALLOWS EASY
ACCESS TO THE DOOR.

The Designer

I Annie Sloan

Few designers can rival Annie Sloan's
expertise with children's furnishings.
Witness her flair for decorative
painting; her interest in designing for
children, which led to the formation of
Hippo Hall (a company which produces
children's bedlinen, fabrics, wallpaper
and furniture), and not least the
influence of her own small sons
(Henry, Thomas and Hugo – aged six,
three and one), which is clearly
evident in her understanding of
children's needs.

At present she is pursuing a
freelance career, writing, painting
murals and teaching art and decorative
techniques to adults and children. She
likes to spend as much time as possible
with her own children, and
consequently works from a studio
attached to the family home in
Oxfordshire, an arrangement ideally
suited to her lifestyle.

Annie believes it is important to
create a welcoming home for children.
Consequently, her colourful paintings
are found in every room of her own
house. The playroom is decorated with
a pear tree mural (which the whole
family helped to print, using a
cornucopia of potatoes, turnips,
mangel wurzels and, for authenticity, a
pear), and picture book animals graze
by the window. In the stencilled
kitchen, the units and even the freezer
are embellished with Annie's bright
and humorous designs. Upstairs, you
will find a trompe l'oeil window,
complete with real curtains, filling a
blank wall at the end of the landing.

Her imaginative, yet practical
approach is well illustrated by the
sponging of baby Hugo's bedroom in a
sunny yellow just before he was

born – a warm colour, appropriate to
the room's northerly aspect and
suitable for children of either sex, so
there wouldn't have been a problem if
the baby had been a girl. Annie plans
to add a border, 'now that he's
beginning to take notice', but will have
to proceed with care because she has
discovered that her vocation has one
major drawback; 'the children see me
painting on the walls so they think that
it's all right for them to do it too', she
says. 'They do some wonderful things,
but it's not what I want on the walls!'

Annie's Design

'Wallpaper is not practical for children's rooms', says Annie with feeling; which is why she opted for a washable, oil-based eggshell paint that will withstand the impact of toy cars and sticky fingers.

Her first step was to paint the entire room white, as a base for a cheap and easy decorative scheme, and one which parents and children could create together. Using only a can of blue, cellulose spray paint (the type

intended for cars), a light touch on the nozzle and a few spare minutes, she transformed the walls into an instant mural of billowing clouds and patches of blue sky (see 'how to create a cloudy sky', page 93).

Next, Annie created a landscape of hills and fields around the base of the walls, by rubbing on diluted green poster paint with crumpled newspaper – a technique called '*frottage*' or 'frotting' (see page 93). By deliberately varying the depth of colour she has introduced a sense of perspective to the mural. This is enhanced by a series of cut-outs – a teddy, a bunch of flowers, trundling cars and floating balloons – all drawn onto white card, coloured in with poster paints and stuck to the walls with glue or Blu-tack. A couple of distant seagulls, drawn in crayon, complete the picture.

Virtually all the materials that Annie used were deliberately chosen because they are readily found in any home where there are young children. This means that it is both easy and inexpensive to add to or vary the design at any time. 'This is something a child might do', says Annie, suggesting that the simple motifs she used could be changed for more sophisticated ones as the child gets older. Indeed, painting in and cutting out simple shapes from white card is an ideal project to keep children amused during the weekend.

Similarly, no expert knowledge is required to wield a spray can or rub on paint with a piece of newspaper. However, Annie does suggest that the spraying is left to the parents, who are advised to open the windows and wear a simple face mask, to avoid inhaling fumes during painting.

To complete the decorations Annie suggested the presence of a few 'dark clouds', by painting a blackboard over the base of the existing cupboard door and by blacking the inside of the fireplace, which has been kept as a storage space cum hidey-hole.

The blue cord carpet blends in with the overall colour scheme. It is cheap, hard wearing and soft enough to sit on, but has a pile which will not impede the movement of wheeled toys. Finally, the matching curtains and

Annie's cloud mural creates a fantasy land for Christopher, but the room's furnishings are practical and robust.

bedding feature nosediving planes to enhance the theme of the room.

Annie chose the sturdy pine furniture primarily to save space. It consists of an L-shaped bunk arrangement, with a desk and storage space for books underneath, plus a small dressing table. The bunks conform to the new government safety regulations, but as an additional precaution young children should sleep in the lower one until they are five. 'The upper bunk is not suitable for a baby, but it will provide an extra bed later on when Christopher has friends to stay', explains Annie. 'Meantime the top bunk makes a playhouse for him underneath – and a climbing frame!'

The additional advantage of this type of furniture is that a small matching chest can be added to the top bunk, if more storage space for clothes is required later on. The total cost was a fairly modest £500, and Annie estimates that the decorating would come to no more than £10 – a down to earth price for a 'heavenly' room.

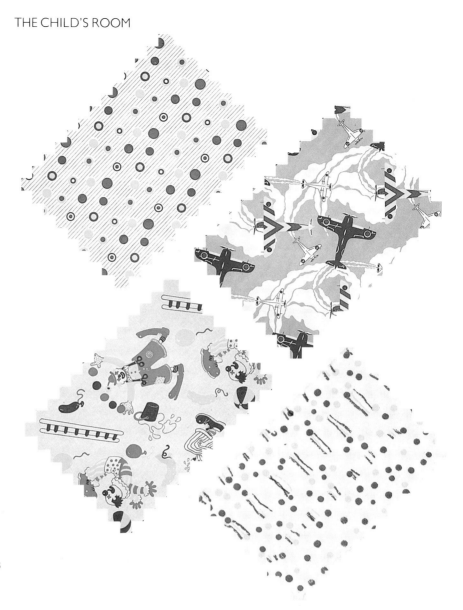

Above right. Aeroplanes and target-patterned paper and fabrics are a lively choice, but some children may prefer the clown designs in an alternative colour scheme of green, red and yellow.

By using furniture of compatible width and depth, Annie was able to fit L-shaped bunks, a desk, a stool and a dressing table into the small room. She has retained the built-in cupboard and the fireplace, which now provides extra storage for toys.

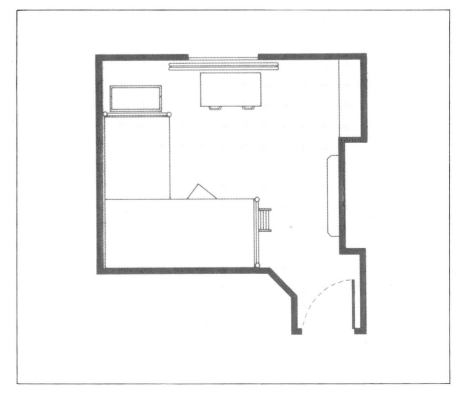

Above. Annie's sketch for a versatile mural, encouraging children to participate by adding their own motifs cut out from card.

Right. The mural is created by spraying blue paint onto a white background to simulate the effect of clouds.

Left. Brightly coloured card is used for the stick-on wall shapes, adding a cheerful accent to the soft green and blue of the mural.

Below. Matt black paint creates an inviting blackboard on the cupboard door and a hidey-hole in the former fireplace.

Creating a Landscape with Frottage

Frottage, or a rubbed finish, is the simple technique used to create the landscape in Annie's mural. It produces a streaky, mottled effect – achieved by rubbing a watery solution of poster paint onto the wall with a few sheets of crumpled newsprint. The paper absorbs just enough of the paint for tonal variation.

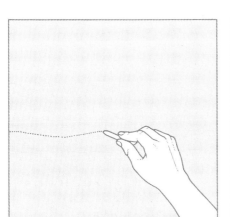

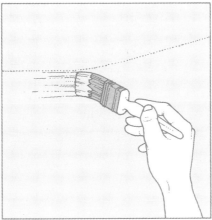

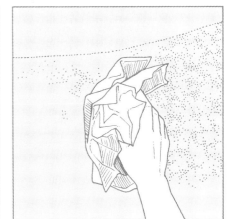

1 Mark out the area to be painted, using soft chalk to create the outlines of the landscape – though this technique is equally effective for seascapes.

2 Make up a well-thinned solution of green poster paint or emulsion (or use brown for earth and blue for water). Apply one coat to the areas within the chalk outlines, using a 5cm (2in) standard paint brush. Let the children help if they want to.

3 Before the paint dries, crumple up a sheet of newspaper and rub and dab it vigorously over the surface. This will displace and remove some of the paint, to produce the streaky, mottled finish. When dry add details such as birds, using crayon or felt tip.

How to Create a Cloudy Sky

Create the effect of blue sky breaking through the clouds, as Annie Sloan has done in Christopher's room, with this quick and easy decorative treatment. It is a very effective starting point for a mural, but as you will be using cellulose-based spray paint, which gives off toxic fumes in a confined space, don't let the children join in at this stage.

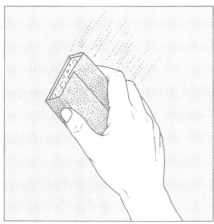

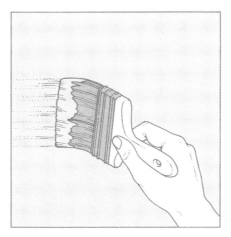

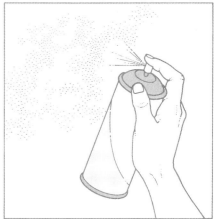

1 Prepare the wall or ceiling by filling any cracks with a proprietary filler. Sand down the surface to provide a key for the base coat. Then clean with a solution of sugar soap, rinse thoroughly and allow to dry.

2 Paint the wall or ceiling with two coats of white eggshell paint. Allow the surface to dry before and after applying the second coat. Then turn off the heating, open windows and doors and put on a face mask (available from most DIY stores).

3 Apply the sky blue aerosol paint, using a light touch on the nozzle and a series of delicate, random movements, to create streaks of blue sky. Don't overdo the spraying or you will spoil the airy effect.

The Designer

2 Jon Lys Turner

A designer in his mid-twenties, Jon Lys Turner has only recently left the Royal College of Art in London. Though first known for his original paint treatments of furniture, his designs gained a wider audience when transferred to T-shirts – which were snapped up by aficionados of style at such fashionable stores as Hyper Hyper and Browns, in London.

Although Jon now creates nightshirts and nightdresses to accompany his collections of bedlinen, his prints have moved on from T-shirts to home textiles, primarily because he does not want to pursue a career exclusively in fashion. He prefers to spend his time designing furnishings and creating interiors – especially for West End stores and restaurants, and affluent and avant-garde private clients, for whom he has decorated many children's rooms.

His work has become identified with the neo-classical style, and his trend-setting designs have proved so acceptable to a wide range of tastes that nowadays his textiles can be seen in mainstream department stores, like Liberty and Peter Jones, as well as various outposts of style such as Soho Designs.

A hallmark of his is the loosely interpreted architectural motif, such as the wobbly Ionic columns which adorn his award-winning range of bedlinen. There is also a pervasive Venetian influence; one of his T-shirts was called 'Tintoretto', and his work is 'full of angels and orgies', he says.

However, Jon has tempered these ideas for two year old Christopher's room, for he is well aware of the limitations furnishings can impose on

the designer. 'People want things to match the curtains and furnishings they brought years ago', he concedes, 'so you have to play safe'.

The small white bed and the Alice in Wonderland chairs play fascinating tricks with perspective in this unusual design with classically-inspired motifs.

Jon Lys Turner's Design

Looking at the room Jon has created for Christopher George is a bit like peering through a fishbowl. For in contrast to the designers who cut the room down to child size, Jon has magnified the furnishings to produce an Alice in Wonderland effect. The looming chairs, towering columns and adult colour scheme ensure that little Christopher will know exactly how Alice in Wonderland felt when she took the bottle marked 'Drink Me'.

Jon deliberately chose furniture which makes no concession to a two year old. 'The brief was to take a child from 18 months into his teens, and at the age of 17 I didn't really see him in a Mothercare chair', he says. The art nouveau style chairs, with their elegant elongated backs, reinforce the element of fantasy and as Jon points out, 'he is as likely to fall off any other chair as these'.

The choice of work surface is equally valid – and just as

controversial. Jon has used a round dining table, at present bearing a display of cartoon figures and some rather expensive tinplate clockwork cars (which many adults would covet), but also intended for children to sit around when playing games or using a computer.

The only other visible items of furniture are the bed, next to the now defunct fireplace, with its head tucked into the alcove which once contained the storage cupboard; a hamper for books and toys, in front of the chimney breast, and a high-tech metal cabinet, which originally held dentist's drills and was a bargain buy at only £30 from Camden Market in London. Stripped of its original, white enamel finish it now holds a collection of antique toys, protected from small prying fingers by glass doors. More accessible is the modern fitted wardrobe, containing all Christopher's clothes, along the wall opposite the fireplace.

The decoration is as sophisticated as the furnishings, but eminently practical. Jon has painted the off-white emulsioned walls with streaky, apricot coloured stripes, to suggest panels, columns and arches (see 'distressed finish', page 98). He has hung prints, which are in fact enlarged photocopies of classic mosaics – the cheap paper having been ripped and stained with tea to resemble old parchment (see 'how to make a photocopy mural', page 99). These pocket money pictures cost little more than £1 each to produce, so the image can be changed every week if desired – and as they are for personal use, the laws of copyright do not apply.

Classical motifs recur on the bedding (one of Jon's own designs), and on the hand-tufted blue rug, which adds the one note of strong colour and has a faintly Byzantine air.

The theme is extended to the lighting by Jon's ingenious use of terracotta wall urns: available from garden centres and originally intended as shrub baskets. He has converted them into stylish uplighters by running a lead through the drainage hole at the back and colouring them with a distressed bronze finish. They mix happily with the white Venetian blind at the window and the modern Tizio desk lamp on the table, giving the room a sense of style which Jon hopes Christopher will grow to appreciate. 'I have avoided all twentieth century children's themes as these are soon outmoded', says Jon. 'My designs were outmoded five hundred years ago!'

Above. Jon's ingenious wall lights are made from terracotta wall urns originally intended for garden use.

Removing the built-in cupboard enables Jon to push the bed right into the alcove, freeing more space for play. Storage is provided by floor to ceiling cupboards across the back wall and by the display cabinet for treasures, salvaged from a dental surgery.

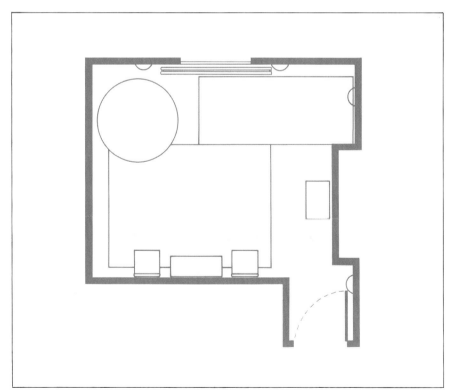

Above and top. Jon's sketch of his panelled wall treatment and the hand-tufted rug, decorated with his own distinctive designs.

Right. The dentist's cabinet with its display of toys is set between the tall chairs for a deliberately formal arrangement.

How to Paint a Distressed Panel Finish

A distressed or 'broken' finish is produced by removing and displacing paint from a surface in order to simulate ageing or wear and tear. Such finishes are used by avant-garde interior designers when they are trying to simulate an air of faded gentility or decay – it being considered chic to simulate crumbling stone or damaged plaster, even if the walls are in good repair!

Whilst the extremes of this technique are not for those who would rather banish than create damp patches and cracked surfaces, it is undeniable that a gently faded look can be far more interesting that a simple coat of emulsion, and much easier to live with than a patterned wallpaper.

The subtle, panelled finish that Jon Lys Turner produced on the walls of Christopher's bedroom is simpler to recreate than appears at first sight.

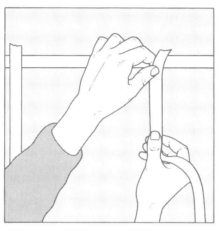

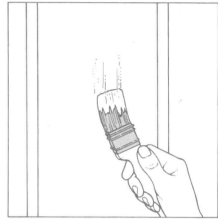

1 Prepare the walls by filling all cracks, rubbing down to key the surface and washing and rinsing. When dry, apply two coats of emulsion paint in the colour of your choice.

2 After the paint has dried, mark out the outlines of the panels with low-tack masking tape. Use a plumb line to ensure that the vertical edges are straight, and a spirit-level to check the horizontals.

3 Paint in the panels, again with the colour of your choice. It is a good idea to choose a colour that won't be too vivid a contrast with the base coat. But, whatever you opt for 'it will look very bright and messy at this stage', warns Jon.

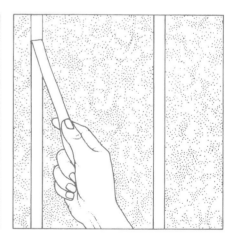

4 When dry, cover the newly painted panels with a mixture of 3 parts white emulsion to 1 part scumble glaze (available from artists' suppliers).

5 Whilst still wet, remove and displace some of the glaze either by rag-rolling it with a bunch of rags, twisted to form a sausage, and a pushing and rolling movement; sponging it with a marine sponge and a dabbing action, or combing it with the serrated edge of a piece of card.

6 When the distressed glaze has dried, carefully peel away the masking tape to reveal the finished panels. At this stage you can embellish the design, as Jon has done, with various motifs painted in freehand.

Jon Lys Turner used photocopies of classical mosaics as the basis of his designs for the pictures in Christopher's room, creating an 'antique fresco' feel for the walls.

How to Turn a Photocopy Into a Mural

Using a photocopier with an enlarging facility is an easy way for you to copy a motif from curtains, bedlinen or upholstery fabrics, and then employ it as a complementary stencil elsewhere in a room.

Jon Lys Turner used this technique to create wall decorations for Christopher's bedroom which resemble antique frescos. Basically, he photocopied and enlarged classical motifs, stained the paper with tea to produce an antique effect, and then stuck them to the wall. However, the method outlined below (a bit like

brass rubbing) is a way of making the position of the motifs rather more permanent. Though there is nothing to stop you sandwiching the enlarged picture between two pieces of glass and a bit of hardboard, held together with clips, and hanging it on the wall. Then you have the option of moving or changing it later on.

1 Select a motif from a book, magazine, or a fabric used elsewhere in the room. (As it's for your own use, the laws of copyright don't apply.) Place it on the photocopier and enlarge it to the required size.

2 Coat the printed side of the photocopy paper with photographic spray mount (open the windows and doors to ensure adequate ventilation). Place it in position, printed side down, on the wall.

3 Brush lighter fuel onto the reverse side, rubbing it in well, to transfer the print to the wall.

The Designer

3 Floella Benjamin

Floella Benjamin, the presenter of children's Play School and Playaway programmes, once worked in a bank. But one career she had not embarked on, until now, was interior design. However, a strong visual sense and an understanding of children made her an obvious choice for Christopher's room, and she is no stranger to the business of decorating, having had ample opportunity to develop her talents while restoring her large Victorian home.

The room she designed for her son Aston (now aged 6), when he was a baby, proved an invaluable testing ground for her theories. Floella believes that children should be surrounded by their possessions and bright, primary colours – confirmed by the shoals of appreciative mail she receives after she wears something especially colourful on Play School.

Consequently, Aston has a fairytale wallpaper in which every picture tells a story ('I didn't want a babyish paper because it had to last a good few years', Floella explains) and, in case his imagination palls, a brightly coloured mural on an adjacent wall. Floella has provided plenty of child size furniture and a generous amount of storage space and shelving; the latter crowded with toys, such as Kermit, Thomas the Tank Engine, a row of teddies and, of course, Humpty from Play School, who all contribute to the decor.

She does admit to having made mistakes. 'One thing I failed on is the carpet', she says. 'Though it's warm and soft it's wrong for older children who need a hard floor for playing on – and carpet costs so much money you can't replace it easily.' However,

Aston shows no sign of dissatisfaction at present.

When he wants a change Floella will be happy to allow him freedom of choice, 'though if he chooses something really bad I'll try to talk him out of it', she says. However she hopes that whatever he rebels with will be something that is pleasant to the eye.

Pattern and primary colours create a stimulating but safety-conscious setting for two year old Christopher.

Floella Benjamin's Design

'It has to be practical, it has to be safe, it has to have storage space and it has to make the child feel as if he wants to be there.' Those were Floella's priorities when designing Christopher's room; a task she set about with confidence because it was similar in period and style to her son Aston's bedroom.

The result is a vivid, cheerful room, decorated in a combination of red, yellow and green offset by white, which shows the importance Floella places on bright colour. Nearly every item repeats the dominant colour scheme: the radiator is painted green, the panelled entrance door is red and yellow, and the multi-coloured shelves, curtained worktop by the bed, bedlinen, lights, cushions and storage bins all take up the theme.

Even the floor is chequered with vibrant red and yellow vinyl tiles. They are practical as well as decorative, because they won't interfere with

wheeled toys, and because they 'create a sense of excitement', by serving as a base for hopscotch or outsize board games.

The focal point of the scheme is the sunshine mural on the chimney breast (Floella filled in the fireplace, which she considers 'a waste of space'), flanked by a plain white wall on one side, and a wallpaper with a teddy and building block design on the other.

Though the room is full of pattern, furniture is kept to a minimum to clear the floor for play. There is a freestanding wardrobe for Christopher's clothes, in the alcove by the chimney breast, and a pine toy chest under the window. A pair of stacking beds, also in pine, means overnight guests can be accommodated. When not in use the second bed is stored underneath the top one, and its mattress used as a backrest. Floella believes this is a far more sensible option than conventional bunk beds, which she feels are unsuitable for young children. 'I went for safety most of all', she says, pointing to the yellow bars fixed across the deep window and the socket covers on each electric point. She also kept to a strict budget. For example, the tiny rugs, held in place with latex glue for safety, cost under £5 and the scarlet blind at the window is a cheap and cheerful roll-up type.

However, the most noticeable aspect of the scheme is Floella's child's eye view: coat pegs are fixed just inside the door at toddler height; brightly coloured stacking crates keep sets of Lego and puzzles intact (and might encourage tidiness), and the mural is designed so that Christopher can draw on the 'sand'. All thoughtful touches which show that Floella has carried out her own dictum to 'Think Child'.

Top. Multi-coloured shelves and a worktop provide an impromptu desk, while the curtain below hides toys and clutter.

Right. Floella's sketch of her mural shows a large beach so that Christopher can add his own artistic touches to the scene.

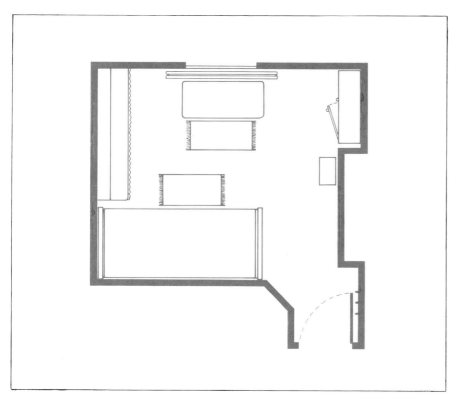

Floella's plan puts the accent on safety, with bars at the windows and stacking beds in place of high bunks. The fireplace is filled in to make way for a mural and the built-in cupboard has been replaced by a modern free-standing version.

Above. Paint in bright primaries is used in abundance to create a dazzling colour scheme.

Red, yellow and green form the basis of a lively scheme where even the door is painted to match the chequered floor.

How to Create a Mural

You can draw simple murals straight on to the wall, like Floella Benjamin, but you may want a more complicated design or even a recreation of a picture from a book or magazine. It could be anything from a simple beach scene to an intergalactic starfleet battle. Unless you happen to be a rather talented fine artist, you may not feel able to reproduce this freehand. So, apart from some of the minor details, you will have to transfer the picture from book to wall by means of a simple grid system.

Although this sounds rather ambitious and somewhat intimidating, in fact it is quite a simple technique that just requires a certain amount of patience. The mural is sketched in square by square and then painted one colour at a time. Obviously, the simpler the picture the easier it is. But even a basic beach scene can make a dramatic impact, as Floella's mural proves. Moreover, greater definition and further interest can be added at the end, by simply outlining some of the features with a felt tip pen and painting freehand a few simple extra details – whether they be small birds flying in the distance or the lasers on a space cruiser.

1 Place grid tracing paper over picture. Using a pencil, trace outline of all the features and details to be included.

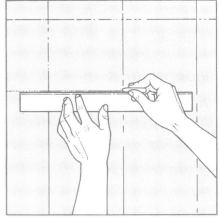

2 Scale up grid to required size (e.g. increase squares by factor of 10) and transfer to wall, using ruler and chalk.

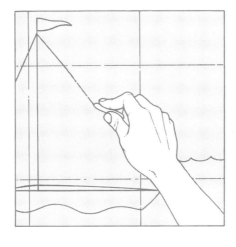

3 Referring to outlines of picture on tracing paper grid, copy one square at a time onto wall grid, using chalk.

4 Working from top, fill in one colour at a time. When dry, rub out chalk and fill in any small extra details freehand.

Tricia and Dermott's Conclusion

Like Goldilocks, the Georges felt that one room was too hard, one was too soft and one was just right for Christopher.

Dermott admired the subtle scheme Jon Lys Turner had created, but felt that it was too restrained and that the inevitable football stickers would soon spoil the effect. 'A child likes more of a muddle', he said. On the other hand, Tricia thought that the nursery wallpaper in Floella's room looked backwards to babyhood, though both of them liked the emphasis on safety and her 'mother's touch'.

The Georges admired the whimsical quality and homely feeling of Annie's scheme most of all. They felt it an ideal setting for Christopher to work, rest and play in, and thought that the whole family could have great fun creating what Dermott described as a 'snug little nest in the treetops'.

As standards of cleanliness rise, the space in which to achieve them dwindles, or so it would seem from the size of the modern bathroom. Sometimes there is compensation in the form of additional facilities, like a downstairs cloakroom or an en-suite shower room, but in the starter homes and flats favoured by first time buyers, the conveniences of basin, bath, shower and w.c. may have to be crowded into a room which measures as little as 2 metres (6ft) square. As our designers will demonstrate, this is not an impossible challenge, but it does require careful planning.

Top of the list of priorities is the need for room to move. There are certain 'rules' you should follow: allow a minimum of 1 metre (approx 3ft) beside the bath and in front of the washbasin to dry yourself in comfort; make sure that the basin and w.c. have 0.5 metre (approx 1½ft) of space on either side to allow sufficient elbow and knee room; if you want to put the basin, w.c. and possibly a bidet along the same wall, allow approximately 70cm (2ft) between each of them, and remember that you will need 80cm (2ft 4in) minimum in front of the bidet and w.c. to, as they used to say on the railways, 'adjust your dress'. To avoid confusion at a later stage, draw the outline of the room onto some squared paper, and mark in the position of the sanitaryware, allowing room for the supply and waste pipes. This should ensure that you will be able to bend over the basin without knocking your elbows on the walls or get out of the bath without putting a foot in the loo!

There are a number of options open to you when trying to make the most of a restricted space. Installing a vanity unit rather than a free-standing basin provides additional storage space and there are ways of keeping down the costs of a complete refit, by utilising existing plumbing. Our designers tackle these problems, and in so doing provide a wealth of ideas to help you plan and decorate your bathroom in a style to suit your taste.

THE ORIGINAL BATHROOM

Despite two incomes, newly weds Simon and Alison Kennedy find their finances severely stretched by the house they are restoring. Simon, a systems analyst, likes to have some say in the decorations, but normally gives way to Alison, a sales promoter, who went to art college. After a busy day at work, the two of them like nothing better than to climb into a hot bath – together.

Simon and Alison Kennedy struggled to find anything positive to say about their existing bathroom. 'Not a space-efficient room' was Simon's restrained verdict on the poky L-shape, created from the space culled from two adjoining rooms. Alison was more distressed by the decor: 'a bright blue suite and flamingos and ducks up the wall isn't the most relaxing environment at the end of a hard day in the office', she complained.

Ideally, Alison would have liked a white suite because 'a strongly coloured suite starts to take over the room'. And Simon, who liked white as well, hankered after a Victorian bath tub – though he doubted there was room for it. Somewhat inconsistently, he proposed a corner bath or a double tub with room for two in its stead. But it seems that even a single bath may be beyond the Kennedy's reach, as they have exceeded their budget for re-wiring, re-plumbing and other restoration work elsewhere in the house, and thus may be forced to keep their shabby old blue suite.

Structural improvements take priority in the Kennedy home. However, one item they were determined to replace was the louvre window, which is draughty, out of character and a security risk (the slats

are easily dislodged). 'The house came with louvres', explained Simon, 'and we are gradually replacing them all with traditional sash windows'.

As for decoration, Simon and Alison prefer simple schemes and graphic designs, disliking anything fussy such as festoon blinds. On the other hand, they don't care for settings that are too clinical, such as wall-to-ceiling tiling, preferring the warmth of natural materials, like their pine towel rail, offset by splashes of colour.

Consequently, they can't wait to get rid of the water lily wallpaper, the utilitarian blue-veined tiles and the dark blue carpet which accompanies them. The only feature they were anxious to retain was the radiator

beneath the window, though even this looks unsatisfactory, as it is pushed to one side to make room for the w.c.

What Simon and Alison really wanted to know was, could this difficult room be designed to include an element of luxury on *their* budget. 'It's all very well going to Texas Homecare and what have you, but it would be nice to see what the alternatives are', says Simon. With limited resources and an awkward room to cope with, it's no wonder they decided to seek professional advice 'before taking the plunge'.

A PATTERNED TILES AND WALLPAPER ADORNED WITH WATER LILIES AND FLAMINGOES COMPETE FOR ATTENTION WITH THE DARK BATHROOM SUITE.

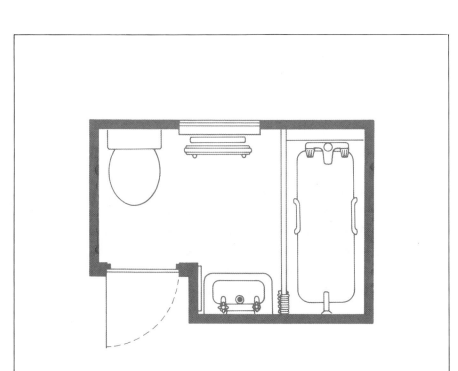

THE BATHROOM WAS CREATED FROM
SPACE CULLED FROM TWO ROOMS IN THE
KENNEDYS' NINETEENTH-CENTURY
TERRACED HOUSE. LUCKILY THE COUPLE
DID NOT WANT A BIDET, FOR THERE IS
HARDLY ROOM FOR THE EXISTING W.C.,
WASH BASIN AND BATH WITH SHOWER.

SIMON AND ALISON REQUESTED A
SCHEME WHICH WOULD BLEND WITH
THEIR EXISTING BATHROOM SUITE IN
CASE THEY COULD NOT AFFORD TO
REPLACE IT. THOUGH RELATIVELY
MODERN, IT HAS NOT WORN WELL AND
THE DEEP COLOUR SHOWS EVERY MARK.

The Designer

1 Doug Patterson

After leaving school at 15, Doug Patterson started out as a Post Office telegraph boy, but at the age of 17 he swapped his BSA Bantam and Velocette Venom for a drawing board in an architect's office. Four years on he transferred to art school, and seven years and four colleges later emerged with an MA from the Royal College of Art and a coveted diploma in architecture from the Architectural Association.

Since then Doug has taken on projects as varied as his initial career. With his partner Jerry Hewitt, he has designed sets for science fiction films, graphics, domestic interiors, and various corporate identities.

When not working for clients like BMW, Alfa Romeo, Granada TV and Lyons Tetley, Doug has found time to convert a dilapidated Methodist chapel and adjoining cottage into his Suffolk home. Plain, light and airy, it is quite different to the schemes demanded by his clients. He has opened it up to form a simple space for everyday living – the walls are white, floors are T & G bordered and sealed, and though it has been virtually rebuilt (having a new roof, dry lined walls and replacement floors) it looks authentically Victorian and a true folly.

In fact, it is an eclectic collection of 'junk' salvaged from the very best demolition sites, including The Savoy apartments, railway stations and 'carefully selected skips'. However, Doug doesn't scorn modern mass production: the charming Gothic windows installed in the cottage, to match those in the chapel, are created by framing up, standard designs from Magnet and Southern.

Inside, the chapel studio is dominated by white columns which draw the eye up the spiral staircase to the balcony, where he has made space for a gallery bedroom and bathroom, which is built into the tower. This pointed, simple room is decorated with bands of grey marble and white

Doug Patterson's Design

Doug has turned the Kennedy's poky little bathroom into a fantasy grotto, complete with shells, statuary, fountain and fish. It's a 'romantic' setting in more ways than one, because he has taken pains to include the corner bath which Simon suggested.

'A corner bath is very practical because it's an economical way of using space', says Doug. But efficiency was not his only concern, for this standard piece of sanitaryware now resembles a fairytale pool decorated with candles and plants, and is surmounted by a shell grotto housing a tame satyr who spouts water into the basin below. 'The effect of running water is very tranquil', comments Doug, who has hidden the one-gallon tank and pump for the fountain in the mirrored cupboard to the right of the bath.

Shells from the Caribbean play an important part in this folly setting: the archway to the grotto is decorated with shells in true rococo fashion (which necessitates some care when rising from the bath!): the design is carried through to the carefully selected wall lights and washbasin which are shell-shaped. Echoed by the corner bath, their curved profiles add a new dimension to an otherwise angular, boxy room.

Further decoration and bolder colour is supplied by tiles. Doug has used more than half a dozen different styles, mixing standard pale blue and white tiles laid in horizontal bands with a cobalt border at picture rail and dado level with two floral designs forming a second banding effect. There are blue mosaics inside the grotto, and an assortment of richly coloured plain tiles and patterned blue ones on the plinth (which conceals the plumbing and provides a shelf for display).

Doug has avoided expensive alterations to the supply and waste pipes where possible. However he has shifted the w.c. along the wall to make room for the shell-shaped basin underneath the new window – a graceful oriel design with cantilevered panes that let in more light. In keeping with its traditional style, Doug has covered the window with a festoon blind, in white to match the full length

tiles, furnished with white sanitary-ware and chrome taps gleaned from The Savoy, and is designed to be practical and easy to clean.

Sea shells of all kinds – real, china and stencilled – plus spouting satyr's head and candelabra turn a tiny bathroom into a fantasy grotto.

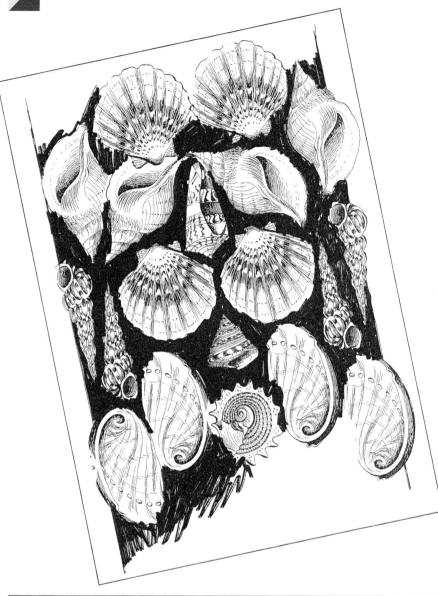

shower curtain, which is tied back with a silver cord to create a theatrical effect at the entrance to the room.

In contrast to the fantasy elements and the wealth of pattern and detail in the scheme, the fittings are simple in style. The towel rails and taps are plain chrome and match the swing-out shaving and make-up mirrors.

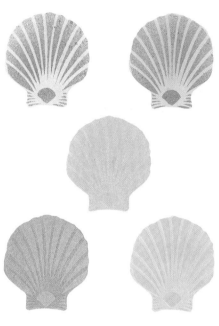

Shells are a recurrent motif in the bathroom Doug has designed for Simon and Alison. A selection of real shells (illustrated above left) is embedded in the entrance to the grotto while stencilled shells (above) decorate the floor.

Although the w.c. remains in its original place opposite the door, the basin has been moved across the room and is now set beneath the window. In its place is a large corner bath complete with grotto which dominates the room.

Visual warmth is added to the scheme by a terracotta vinyl floor, embellished with stencilled shells painted pink. 'Real' warmth is provided by the heated towel rails on either side of the basin, which Doug installed to replace the radiator – the one designer who decided against using the Victorian towel horse.

The bathroom is now, as Doug admits, 'quite a decorative space to be in'. But though it might be an over-the-top scheme, it is not an excessively expensive one. The sanitaryware, including the sumptuous corner bath, costs around £850, and as Doug points out, this is a DIY bathroom. 'Anyone could construct it', he says – which

might be more advisable than asking a builder – there aren't too many used to styling rococo grottos.

A flouncy festoon blind and bathroomware in white offset the boldly patterned tiles which conceal the plumbing.

How to build a rococo style archway

Doug Patterson's shell archway and grotto is the focal point of his bathroom scheme. Doug has furnished his grotto with a gargoyle water spout, circulated by a concealed electric pump; the illumination is via concealed spotlights. While the electrical and plumbing arrangements involved in such a setting are complicated, DIY enthusiasts could quite easily arrange the components. Plants or ornaments inside complete this bizarre display. In fact the technique for making the archway, which is described below, is just as effective for making a mirror surround, and need not be confined to the bathroom.

Below left. The water in the fountain is constantly recirculated by a pump concealed in the cupboard to the left.

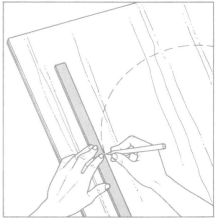

1 Transfer dimensions of space where arch is to be sited to a standard 2.4 by 1.2 m (8 by 4 ft) sheet of marine plywood. Using pencil, straight edge and freehand, mark out outline of arch, and cut out with jig saw.

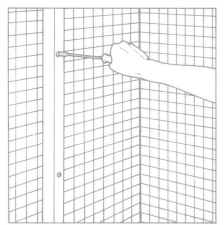

2 Hold arch in position, and mark position of edges on (tiled) wall. Cut out two 5 by 5 cm (2 by 2 in) battens, to length, and plane down leading edges to sit flush with back of arch. Screw battens to wall and archway to battens.

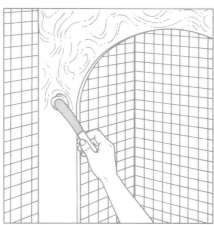

3 Having sealed screw heads with metal primer, and sealed board with yacht lacquer, mix up a batch of fibreglass quilting and resin (available from car accessory shops, with instructions) and cover arch with this 'stucco' mix. Use spatula to distress surface.

4 Either stick shells to surface while still wet, or seal dry surface with lacquer and stick shells on with water-resistant adhesive. Finally, paint uncovered stucco to match decor and fill grotto with plants, glass shelving, decorative objects etc . . .

The Designer

2 Althea Wilson

Somewhere between Africa, England and a Swiss school, Althea Wilson acquired a passion for the Tudors and Stuarts, which inspired the conversion of her own nineteenth-century home into a facsimile of a Jacobean manor house – complete with panelled hall and carved cupboards in the kitchen. But, Althea goes further than most exponents of 'retro chic'. She confesses to being obsessed with the period, sleeping in a Jacobean four-poster and filling the house with period items.

An artist since childhood (her first exhibition was in Nigeria at the age of 15), it is only in the past few years that she has concentrated on interior design. Prior to that she dealt in antiques, an experience which equipped her with the knowledge and contacts required to invest shrewdly in pieces for her own home, such as a seventeenth-century four-poster and a Charles II chinoiserie cabinet, which will some day 'provide my old age pension'.

However, Althea has never stopped painting, as the portraits that decorate the walls of her home show (neighbours complain they make the house look like an extension of the National Portrait Gallery). Her main bathroom is a stunning combination of Victorian sanitaryware and Renaissance trompe l'oeil, incorporating a painted stone wall bearing plants and urns which turn the windowless space into a room with a view – evidence of her talent for paint techniques, a subject on which she has just written her own book.

Elsewhere the pre-Augustan influence is undiluted. Her bedroom is dominated by the four-poster, and a

decorative stencilled frieze runs round the walls. It is an opulent but faded look that is repeated in the textiles – even the duvet cover looks like damask. And are the curtains in her sitting room faded Italian silk? 'No', she says, 'they're Peter Jones' best'. Like the portraits she creates for friends who own Tudor mansions but can't afford sixteenth-century fine art to match, they are evidence that her approach to interior design is more practical than it might seem.

Long-legged flies and moths drift across the tiles, bath panel and vanity unit doors in a design which combines the colour of delftware with the style of traditional crewel work.

Althea Wilson's Design

'In my experience, nobody ever gets tired of blue and white', says Althea Wilson, explaining her choice of a scheme based on seventeenth-century delftware designs. Whilst she sympathizes with Alison and Simon's wish to replace their blue suite with a white one, she believes her plan is flexible enough for them to retain it if finances won't stretch to a new one – which in this case cost only £200.

To make better use of the confined space, Althea has turned the position of the bath through ninety degrees so that now it is opposite the window. A false wall has been built in to accommodate the length of the bath and to provide a semi-enclosed shower area; though Althea suggests a shower curtain or glass panel might be needed to stop water spraying onto the floor.

The basin has changed places with

the bath and now is set into a purpose-made vanity unit. This helps to create an air of luxury difficult to achieve in small bathrooms, and the adjustable shelving inside provides much needed storage space.

The most eye-catching elements of the scheme are the painted insects and flowers, inspired by antique crewel work which Althea, a skilled needlewoman, admires. A swarm of long-legged insects hovers over bath and basin, while snails and stylized tulips are found closer to the ground on the bath panel and vanity unit doors, and the design spills over on to the white roller blind. Not for those whose worst nightmares concern the spider in the tub, but Althea vouches for the pattern's popularity. 'They used a lot of insects in Queen Anne's time, and I found that customers were always asking for them, so they became part of my style', she says.

Althea used standard glazes to paint the designs on to the white tiles, which were subsequently fired to set the design. She has restricted the tiling to the wall above the bath, the bath panel and the basin splashback, partly to cut costs (these elegant tiles cost £5 each), and partly because she likes the contrast between matt and shiny surfaces. The rest of the wall area is sponged in blue and white, to produce a restful effect, and the floor is covered with a budget price blue-grey vinyl, which resembles ceramic tiles at a fraction of the cost.

There's little room for furniture and accessories, so Althea has restricted these to an antique cane chair with an attractive oval back and a decorative mirror, both colour-rubbed in blue to tie in with the overall scheme. She has provided extra lighting over the mirror with a tungsten tube shielded by a chrome

baffle, and retained the Victorian-style towel horse because its decorative appearance suits the scheme.

Althea believes it's a setting that would complement the original blue suite as successfully as the new white one. It was designed specifically so that Alison and Simon could pick out the elements they like, or can afford. 'In no way will it spoil the ultimate effect if they can't afford the complete design', Althea insists. For example, 'you can have many (painted) tiles or few', depending on your budget.

It all adds up to an elegant scheme which is light, airy and, as Althea points out, easy to keep clean – yet another example of the pragmatic attitude which accompanies her decorative talent.

Left. Flowers and beetles are found appropriately close to the ground. Their colour is repeated in the colour-rubbed cane chair and mirror frame.

Right. A blue tiled band at dado level adds a fresh contrast to the predominantly white tiles and white sanitaryware. Walls are tiled to full height behind the bath but elsewhere are sponged in blue on white for softness.

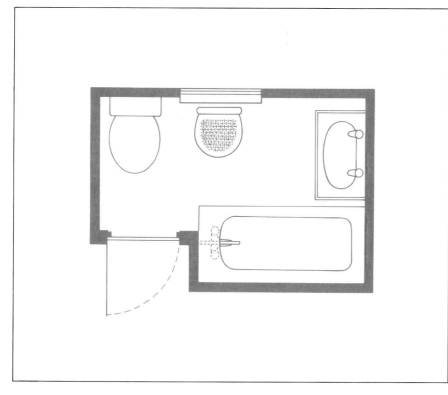

To increase floor space, Althea has moved the bath to the wall opposite the window and boxed it in to provide a shower screen. The basin is set into a vanity unit to provide extra storage space.

How to Colour Rub Furniture

The oval-backed cane chair and decorative mirror in Althea Wilson's bathroom were colour rubbed in blue to match the overall scheme.

Colour rubbing, another of the 'distressed' finishes so popular with designers today, involves rubbing emulsion paint into the surface of an object, thereby throwing any contours and mouldings into relief and emphasising the play of light and shade over the surface. For this reason it is best applied to ornate decorative pieces (carved furniture is ideal), and is also suitable for cast iron fireplaces, cornices, picture rails and relief wallcoverings.

Because the technique depends partly on rubbing colour *off* (as well as in), choose fairly deep shades, rather than light colours and soft pastels, or the effect may be lost. But avoid *very* dark colours, as they will produce too strong a contrast.

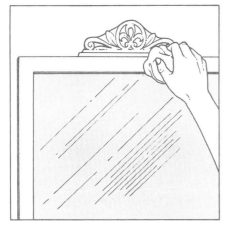

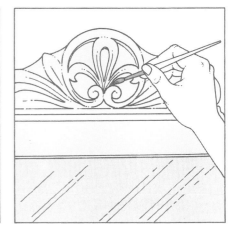

1 Prepare surface: clean bare wood with white spirit, remove waxed finish with methylated spirits, and rub down painted surfaces with wet and dry paper. Clean thoroughly and allow to dry. Use an old toothbrush to clean out crevices, if necessary.

2 Having applied a coat of primer to bare wood, paint on an undercoat followed by two coats of white emulsion.

3 Take the paint colour of your choice – Althea used blue – and, using a small brush, apply to the piece, brushing it well into the crevices.

4 When the paint is slightly tacky, but still wet, rub it gently, in a circular motion, using a flat, clean car or horse sponge. It's counter-productive to work the sponge into the crevices as this will destroy the effect. So, just rub lightly over the mouldings.

5 The excess paint will come away on the sponge, throwing the contours and mouldings into relief, and producing a shadow effect in the contrast between lighter and darker areas of paint.

6 When dry, apply two or three coats of Beeswax or Antique wax polish, for protection. Leave dull or rub up for extra shine when dry.

These delicate insects are typical of Althea Wilson's style, but are not for those afraid of spiders in the bath!

How to Paint Ceramic Tiles

Althea paints her elegant insect and plant motifs on to plain white tiles, using ready-mixed glaze (Harrison & Mayer 'Onglaze' available from artists' suppliers). When the paint has dried she fires the tiles in a kiln. Commercial firing is an uneconomic prospect for one-off DIY work, but it is worth arranging to rent space in a kiln owned by a local school or college.

If you have no access to a kiln, or if you wish to decorate tiles that are already in position on the wall, it is possible to paint them with ceramic tile paint (available from specialist decorator's shops). However, this will not adhere to the surface as well as fired glaze and, if subjected to steam or water, will need to be protected with a ceramic sealant, or a non-yellowing varnish such as Translac (both available from specialist decorator's shops).

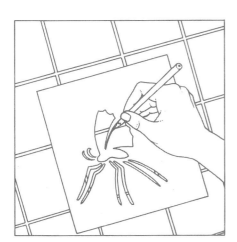

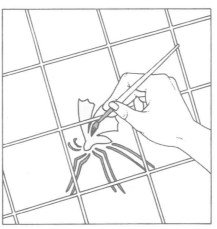

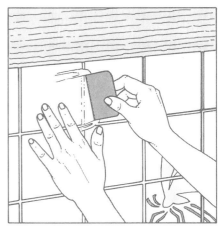

1 Assuming they are new tiles not yet fixed in position, number and lay the tiles on the floor in the same sequence they will be in on the wall (and allow for grout lines). Sketch or stencil (see page 34) the outline of your design onto the tiles.

2 Now paint or stencil the design, using the ready-mixed glaze. Allow to dry and then fire in a kiln. If working on old tiles already fixed in position: wash with mild fungicide solution, rinse, dry and then apply the design with ceramic paint.

3 Fix kiln-fired tiles in position on wall, using waterproof grout, in same numbered sequence as on floor. Ceramic painted tiles should be sealed with two coats of ceramic sealant or Translac non-yellowing varnish, for protection.

The Designer

3 Mary Fox Linton

'Fox Linton Associates are a company of designers rather than decorators', explains Mary. In thirty years they have grown from a small consultancy to an international design organisation, handling such exclusive projects as Chelsea Wharf overlooking the Thames – one of the most expensive housing developments in the world.

However, Mary makes her style accessible to the general public via her shop, which sells furniture, textiles, rugs and china, and she is still happy to tackle domestic commissions. Though Simon and Alison's bathroom is rather smaller than the projects she normally undertakes, her cool, elegant style is equally at home in a terraced house as in millionaire's row.

Mary's own home is at the top of a large Victorian house in Clapham, London. She has turned a series of seven attic rooms into a vast galleried living space, large enough to accommodate a full-size fig tree and, as Mary confides, 'a very good place for a party'. Set in a mist-grey, white and cream colour scheme, an enormous sandstone fireplace ('found hanging in a considerable state of disrepair on the outside wall of a château'), Marcel Brewer chairs, an acrylic table and huge armoire sit happily together. However, although Mary likes mixing old and new, she ruthlessly rejects any object which doesn't contribute to an overall scheme, and feels that limiting the number of decorative pieces in a setting increases their impact.

Perhaps this explains why she likes her bathroom best. 'It hasn't got anything in it which isn't essential', she says. It contains only white sanitaryware, a few pictures and a

curtain beneath the basin to conceal clutter – a scheme dictated not only by Mary's style, but by the room's size.

Mary doesn't believe lack of space is an intractable problem. 'All a bathroom needs is enough cupboard space to put things away, so when you get up in the morning and you're half asleep you know just where to go to find them'; and a sense of calm, 'because if you've had a frantic day, it's nice to have somewhere to relax'.

Creamy carpet and wallcovering teamed with white blinds and bathroomware create a soothing and elegant scheme.

Mary Fox Linton's Design

Elegance and tranquillity are the keynotes of the bathroom Mary has designed for Simon and Alison. It's a scheme based on white and cream which makes the most of the limited space and seems to fill the room with light, not least because Mary has chosen a white Venetian blind for the window, to filter as well as exclude natural light.

The slender 16mm ($\frac{1}{2}$ inch) slats of the microblind are ideal for such a small room, and cover the entire window area from floor to ceiling, effectively concealing the offset radiator. Mary has hung matching blinds either side of the bath, which not only add symmetry and continuity but also have a practical purpose. The blind on the right hides the functional white shower curtain, while that on the left covers the shelves behind the bath which, Mary suspects, will support a rather less than aesthetic assortment of bath oil, soap and shampoo bottles.

Mary had no hesitation in replacing the original blue suite with modern white sanitaryware, the smooth contours of which add to the sense of space. She opted for a pressed steel bath rather than the more usual acrylic, which she dislikes; and by sticking to the original layout has utilised the existing plumbing connections to keep down costs. However, the basin is now set into the

large worktop of a wall-mounted vanity unit – thereby providing extra storage space.

Further storage is provided by unobtrusive glass shelves, set in a tiled alcove built at the end of the bath; and by a cupboard created in the space above the boxed-in w.c. cistern. The latter, papered to match the walls in a creamy geometric design (which adds interest without 'closing down the space'), is virtually undetectable, yet provides a sizeable unit which will store all the toiletries and cleaning materials that the Kennedys would require.

The wallpaper is continued on the side of the bath, where it meets a suede effect carpet in the same honey colour, which has the look and feel of wool but is in fact a synthetic which will resist water (and, unlike wool, won't smell like a wet dog when splashed!). An essential component of Mary's scheme is the subtle contrast between different textures and shades of white and cream; the cool, shiny white of the bathroom suite, blinds, shower curtain and tiles is offset by the

Above and below. Boxing in the cistern makes space for a wall cupboard, equipped with shelves to match those at the head of the bath. The window and radiator are concealed by a white Venetian blind which matches those used to screen the glass shelves and the shower.

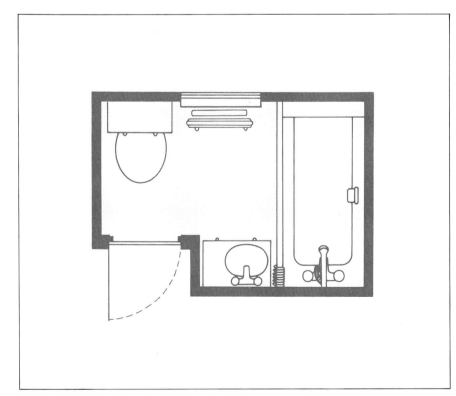

Mary uses the existing plumbing to reduce the cost of installing a new bathroom but has replaced the basin with a vanity unit.

rougher (and warmer) texture and deeper, creamier colour of the patterned wallpaper and carpet.

Mary has kept accessories to a minimum. Carefully chosen pieces of frosted glass for the shelving and a large mirror over the vanity unit reflect the light and help to increase the impression of space. For artificial

light, she has provided chrome spotlights which complement the simple chrome and white basin taps and bath/shower mixer. Even the towels are white, and their deep fluffy pile adds another warm texture to offset the gleaming sanitaryware and tiles. Mary has chosen to drape them over the Kennedy's Victorian-style

clothes horse – the one decorative piece of equipment in the room – adding a traditional touch to a soft and sophisticated modern scheme.

How to Paint on Glass

If you have decided to use glass shelving in your bathroom, as Mary has

done in the Kennedy's, but you would like an alternative to simple plain glass, you can always use a simple paint technique to decorate the shelves.

The simple method described below combines 'flicking' and 'spattering' to produce a frosted look.

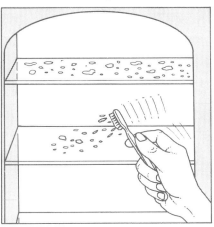

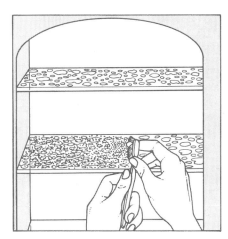

1 Wash the glass thoroughly in soapy water, rinse and dry, then wipe down with methylated spirit and a lint-free rag.

2 Mix up 2 parts of white enamel to 1 part hardener (available from artists' suppliers) and leave to thicken for 20 minutes. Dip an old toothbrush into the enamel and flick your wrist hard so that a shower of drops spatters onto the glass.

3 Repeat step 2 until the glass is covered and leave to dry for at least 24 hours. Then repeat step 2 with a second batch of enamel, but this time run your finger over the bristles to produce a random fine spray. Use two tones of colour for a subtle effect.

Alison and Simon's Reaction

Alison and Simon were astounded by Doug Patterson's scheme, which was more flamboyant than they had expected. Alison liked the new window and the way the room had been reshaped, though Simon was a little uncertain about the shells, which reminded him of ashtrays.

Similarly, the motifs in Althea Wilson's design proved troublesome because neither of them liked dragonflys. And though Alison appreciated the neat vanity unit, she objected to the way the bath had been

enclosed 'in a corridor'.

They felt most at home with Mary Fox Linton's elegant setting. 'I would never have thought of choosing an all-white scheme', confessed Alison, and 'the style is unlikely to date' suggested Simon – not that this will, after all, bother the Kennedys. They are now prospective parents and require a larger home. It's a move they hadn't anticipated – but that's what comes of sharing a bath!

List of Suppliers

Living Room

David Hicks

Paint: Dulux Matchmaker no. 1497 Sulphur. Tel: 0753-31151.

Carpet: Tretford Cord, £14sq m approx, centre of room colour 523, border colour 534, Lynn Lane, Stenstone, Lichfield, Staffs. Tel: 0534-480577.

Sofa: £655; 2 glass-topped Parsons tables £78.35 each; chest squab cushion £54 from David Hicks, 101 Jermyn Street, London, W1. Tel: 01-629-4400. Covering fabric 'Griffin No. 1', £25.75m from Osborne & Little, 304 Kings Road, London, SW3. Tel: 01-352-1456.

Regency chairs: £210, from David Hicks covered in traditional English ticking grey/white, £7.50m, from Ian Mankin, 109 Regents Park Road, London, NW1. Tel: 01-722-0997.

Cushions: £8 from David Hicks (address as above), covered in Majis fabric from Bakers, £19m.

Piccadilly lamps: £175 each and shades £12.50 each, perspex cube £132.85 from David Hicks (address as above).

Curtains: lined and interlined, £418, in cotton fabric 23/4 £4m, from David Hicks (address as above).

Venetian blinds: White metal perforated to order from Tidmarsh, 1 Laycock Street, London, N1. Tel: 01-226-2261.

Cotton tablecloth: fabric no 1237/1 £4m from David Hicks (address as above).

Accessories: small candlestick lamps, vases, pots, boxes and pictures from David Hicks (address as above).

Miscellaneous: Grey Petersham ribbon running round top of wall, Argent 14, £13 per roll from David Hicks (address as above).

Colin Fredricson

Paint: finish by Paul Knowles. Tel: 01-980-9935

Carpet: Palace Velvet Axminster in Vanilla, approx. £18sq m from Brinton's Carpets, PO Box 16, Kidderminster, Worcs, DY10 1AG. Tel: 0562-8200.

Wood floor (lower level): Beech Joker, Campbell Marson, Unit 34, Wimbledon Business Centre, Riverside Road, London, SW17. Tel: 01-897-1909.

Sofa: E20, £236 and armchair, £169, from Estia (range of budget sofas and chairs available with wide choice of fabrics for zip-off covers) 5-7 Tottenham Street, London, W1. Tel: 01-636-5957.

Black cushions: John Lewis, Oxford Street, London, W1 and branches.

Floor to ceiling stacked glass sculpture: designed by Danny Lane, around £8,000 to order from Glassworks, 55-60 Metropolitan Works, Enfield Road, London, N1. Tel: 01-254-9096.

Firescreen: made of glass and wire, designed by Danny Lane, around £600 to order from Glassworks (address as before).

Recessed uplighters (in fireplace): Hoffmeister Lighting, Unit 4, Preston Road, Reading. Tel: 0734-866941.

Glass shelves: Chelsea Glass, 650 Portslade Road, London, SW8. Tel: 01-581-2501.

Tay coffee table: £99, from Habitat, 196 Tottenham Court Road, London, W1 and branches.

Blinds: white venetian, Sunway, Mersey Industrial Estate, Heaton, Mersey, Stockport, SK4 3EQ Tel: 061-432-5303.

Black obelisks: £15.99 each, black figure £32.99, black vases £4.99 to £9.99, cream silk cushions £14.99 each from the Coloroll Store, 156 Regent Street, London, W1. Tel: 01-434-0784.

Miscellaneous: Solitaire, small black glass vase, large black vase with cream line detail and matching fruit bowl from Heals, 196 Tottenham Court Road, London, W1 and branches.

Susy Smith

Paint: Crown Colour Cue, H1-4p Crayfish, T1-5p Niagara Mist, T2-2T Grey Dawn, J1-1P. Tel: 0254-74951.

Floor: Beech Joker £27.50sq m. From Campbell Marson Ltd. Unit 34, Wimbledon Business Centre, Riverside Road, London, SW17. Tel: 01-879-1909.

Dhurry: £189 from a selection at Heals, 196 Tottenham Court Road, London, W1 and branches.

Montgomery sofa: £595, covered in Natural Dobby, £8.45m, and footstool £145 from Laura Ashley, 183 Sloane Street, London, SW1 and branches. Tel: 01-235-9728.

Coffee table: dual purpose, with columns designed by Susy Smith constructed in MDF and painted in Crayfish H1-4P from Crown Colour Cue Range, (address as above).

Pelham wing chair: covered in grey tiger stripe fabric, £509.95 from Heals (address as above).

Fireplace mouldings: Newson's Timber Merchants, 61 Pimlico Road, London, SW1. Tel: 01-730-6262.

Firescreen: designed and painted by Helen O'Keefe for around £110, each is a one-off (she will also undertake commissions to paint furniture, large folding screens, murals and fabrics). Tel: 01-370-7659.

Chest squab cushion: covered in Apricot Chintz, £7.95m from Laura Ashley (address as above).

Curtains and Roman blinds: Rufflette.

Curtains: Traditional English ticking grey/white from Ian Mankin, £7.50m. Tie backs and pelmet in Apricot Chintz, £7.95m, trimmed with bias binding in Smoke from Laura Ashley (address as above). Ian Mankin, 109 Regents Park Road, London, NW1. Tel: 01-722-0997.

Blinds: Perforated Silk Noil fabric £6.80m from Ian Mankin, edged with Smoke webbing from Laura Ashley (address as before).

Spice lampbases: £15.95 each and grey and terracotta Coolie shades £6.95 each from Habitat, 196 Tottenham Court Road, London, W1 and branches.

Terracotta painted pots: designer's own.

Miscellaneous: Soda syphon, £37; Chicago decanter, £26.50; desk flask, £30; Odeon clock, £45.95; blue sponged bowls – small £5.95, large £10.50; pink crackle vase, £24.95, selection of Caleca china, glasses, planters, glass candlesticks from Heals (address as before).

Miscellaneous: Peach cups, saucers and plates (on table), and Cafetiere coffee pot, peach, blue and cream cushions, framed print (above fireplace) all from John Lewis, Oxford Street, London, W1 and branches.

Kitchen

Roy Ackerman

Paint: walls, Dulux Rose white emulsion, Tel: 0753-31151.

Stencilling (in poster paints on walls & blind): by Francesco Pinna and Tony Weller (POA), Tel: 01-627-8648 and 01-376-5127.

Floor: design Amtico 23. Tel: 0203-688771.

Microwave oven 4076, fridge 617D and washing machine WH1025: Electrolux, Luton, Bedfordshire, LU4 9QQ.

Built-in oven HBE 632 & Hob NET 413W: Bosch, PO Box 98, Broadwater Park, North Orbital Road, Denham, Uxbridge, UB9 5HJ.

Marbled bar & worktop: built by Dermot McBride (POA), Unit F21. Action Business Centre, School Road, London, NW10. Tel: 01-961-9291. Paint finish by Francesco Pinna and Tony Weller (address as above).

Sinks and taps: B & Q DIY branches throughout UK.

Wall units (in sink area): Apex budget white wall units from Texas Homecare, Haringey Arena, Green Lanes, London, N4 and branches.

Squab seating & cushions: made in Designer's Guild striped fabric, about £20m, from Swags, Studio 23, Abbey Business Centre, 15–17 Ingate Place, London, SW8 3NS.

Table, chairs, lamps and pictures: loaned by designer.

Solid fuel burning stove: Cream Jotul no. 3, £633, from the London Stove Centre, 49 Chiltern St, London, W1. Tel: 01-486-5168.

White ceiling fan: 'Belaire', £135 at Fantasia, 5 Station Square, Petts Wood, Orpington, Kent, BR5 1LY. Tel: 0689-74044.

Rollerblind: in buttermilk by Sunstor. Tel: 0705-750212

Terrine Bec mixing bowl, wooden spoons, tongs, spatulas, wire egg basket, copper saucepans: Covent Garden Kitchen Supplies, 3 North Row, The Market, Covent Garden, London, WC2. Tel: 01-836-9167.

White fruit bowl, white milk jug: General Trading Company, 144 Sloane St, London, SW1. Tel: 01-730-0411.

Other china & accessories: designer's own.

Potted palms & hanging baskets: Clifton Nurseries, Clifton Villas, Warwick Avenue, London, W9. Tel: 01-289-6851.

Pedro Guedes

Paint: from Berger, Colorizer range,. Nos., 2109, 2105, 3404, 3708, 3810, 2709, 4103, 1903, 307, 3401, 3705, 1010, 4106, 3205, 4206, 305, 301, 1805 emulsions. Tel: 0373-65151.

Floor: Natural sealed cork tiles, from B & Q DIY branches throughout the UK.

Gas hob GH87G, oven FM21, fridge freezer ZF77/33M & washing machine WD 1012: Zanussi Dept. 2K30, Zanussi House, Hambridge Road, Newbury, RG14 5EP. Tel: 0635-512313.

Sideboard (custom built, building sponsored by Zanussi): Zanussi (address as above).

wood, glue, pins & screws from Sainsbury's Homebase. Tel: 01-773-3155.

drawers, knobs, fittings and foldaway ironing-board £65.70 from Woodfit, Kem Mill, Whittle-le-Woods, Chorley, Lancs. PR6 7EA. Tel: 02572-66421.

MDF board from G. H. Buttle & Co., Soothouse Spring, St Albans. Herts, Tel: 0727-34242.

Worktop: Rose Perrino granite, about £20sq ft from W. H. Fraley & Sons, Continental Wharf, Gas Street, Birmingham, B1 2JY. Tel: 021-643-0617.

Lighting: Rise & fall suspension unit £12.95, with Opal glass shade white anglepoise lamps £7.95 each from Habitat, 196 Tottenham Court Road, London, W1 and branches.

Sink: K29, slop bowl and steel tray, approx £200, from GEC Anderson Ltd, 89 Herkomer Road, Bushey, Herts. Tel: 01-950-1826.

White ceramic tiles (in sink area): taps & white melamine shelving from B & Q DIY (address as above)

Shelf supports: versatile white 'Cliffhanger', in 2 & 6ft lengths to cut to size from Woodfit (address as above).

Spaghetti jars, storage jars, labelled spice jars, pestle & mortar, vinegars, mustards: Heals, 196 Tottenham Court Road, London, W1.

Plain spice jars, storage jars, terracotta spice jars, cheese board and chopping block: Habitat (address as above).

Cream fruit bowl: £17.95, from Habitat (address as above).

Miscellaneous: beans, lentils, spices, pasta, jars of olives, peanut butter and honey from Neal's Yard, 21–23 Shorts Gardens, London, WC2. Tel: 01-836-5151.

Lynn Davis

Paint: walls – Dulux matchmaker 1429. Tel: 0753-311511. Units – Colourfast, International Paint. Tel: 01-847-4494.

Floor: White pigmented beech from Junckers £27sq. m. Worktops in same wood available in a range made in sizes from 1.2m long × 625mm wide, £83, up to 3·6m × 625mm wide, £250. Oiling the worktops is recommended – white oil £8.50 per ¾ltr can.

Kitchen units: Sandell Perkins specially constructed for the programme. Sizes available & prices including white melamine doors are: base units: 300mm/£105, 400mm/£112, 500mm/£120, 600mm/£128, 800mm/£167, 1m/£183 & 1.2m/£199. wall units: 300mm/£90, 400mm/£96, 500mm/£104, 600mm/£112, 800mm/£149, 1m/£170. From 22 Praed Street, London, W2 1NH. Tel: 01-258-3922.

Table and chairs: table £160. chairs £195 each from Pearl Dot Furniture, 2 Roman Way, London, N7. Tel: 01-609-3169.

Oven HBE 632, hot NET 413W, dishwasher S5qo, Freezer GIL 1330, Fridge KFR 1830, washing machine V454, tumble drier T445: From Bosch, PO Box 98, Broadwater Park, North Orbital Road, Denham, Uxbridge, UB9 5HH.

Sink and taps: B & Q DIY Branches throughout UK.

Painting (hanging on wall): around £800 by Harland Miller. Tel: 01-734-3961.

Decorative painting (on units): by Harland Miller (address as above).

Ironing board: retractable, (lift mechanism for board by British Gas Springs), approx £125, to order from Grey Matter, 94 Leonard Street, London, EC2. Tel: 01-729-0072.

Cordless iron: Tefal £34.75.

Miscellaneous: Tea towels, oven glove, apron, small white bowls, tea, white mugs with grey dots, casserole, bain marie, saucepans, plastic implements, Arthur Wood storage jars, glass storage jar, wood breadboard, Bistro tea pot & cups, metal sieve, whisk and ladle and grater from Heals, 196 Tottenham Court Road, London, W1.

Chrome fruit bowl, salt and pepper on worktop, glass vase and aperitif glasses: (on table), Authentics, 42 Shelton Street, Covent Garden, London, WC2. Tel: 01-240-9845.

Plates, cutlery, glasses & glass jug (on table) from Habitat, 196 Tottenham Court Road, London, W1.

Clothes (in laundry basket): from Mothercare.

Dining Room

Cebuan de la Rochette

Woodwork: Dulux Matchmaker 1275 Ivory emulsion. Tel: 0753-31151.

Cornice moulding edge: painted with Ardenbrite metallic paint no. 4, Orange, 15 Farringdon Road, London, EC1. Tel: 01-405-2487.

Moiré wallpaper: £9.25 per roll, from Sanderson, 52 Berners Street, London, W1. Tel: 01-636-7800.

Seagrass flooring: £10.95 sq m, from Crucial Trading, P. O. Box 689, London, W2. Tel: 01-727-3634.

Glass table top and shelves: approx £500 to order, from Preedy Glass, Preedy House, Ashland Place, Paddington Street, London, W2. Tel: 01-935-3988.

Shagreen covered legs with cutlery drawers: designed by Cebuan de la Rochette, approx £450 each. Tel: 01-727-0219.

Metal and rattan dining chairs: designed by Cebuan de la Rochette approx £250 each. As before.

Variegated gold mirror panel for door: approx £175 to order (includes measuring, cutting and fitting) from Sekon Glassworks. 301 Business Design Centre, 52 Upper Street, London, N1. Tel: 01-288-6049.

Iridia wall lights: £195 each from Mr Light, 275 Fulham Road, London, SW10. Tel: 01-352-7535.

Low voltage recessed downlights for china display: by Ecro Lighting, 38 Dover Street, London, W1. Tel: 01-408-0321.

Candelabra, glass vase, giant clam shell: designer's own.

Curtains: leather covered poles and curtain making by Purdie & Dewitt in silk organza no. 5201 £2.50m from Pongees. Leather approx £1.25sq ft from Alma Leathers for curtain poles and covered shelves. Purdie & Dewitt, Unit 207, Belgravia Workshops, Marlborough Road, London, N19. Tel: 01-272-6991. Pongees, 184–186 Old Street, London, EC1. Tel: 01-253-0428. Alma Leathers, 17–26 Wakley Street, London, EC1. Tel: 01-278-4343.

Curly willow twigs and antheriums (bird of paradise): from Moyses Stevens.

Colin Gold

Paint on walls: effect achieved with Dulux Matchmaker emulsions 1166 and 1189 and Serenade. Tel: 0753-31151.

Stencilling: by Robert O'Dea who will undertake commissions for special paint effects and stencilling. Tel: 01-582-1367.

Table: made by Sue Wardle Interiors – a budget version as requested by the designer. The top is MDF and the round bases are made of heavy duty packaging tubes cut to size from Curran Packing with dowelling to create the corrugated effect. Painted with coach paint in Standard Red from J. W. Bollom. Sue Wardle Interiors, 14 Grove Hall Court, Hall Road, London, NW8. Tel: 01-286-2457. Curran Packing, Tel: 0375-857131. J. W. Bollom, 13 Theobalds Road, London, WC1. Tel: 01-242-0313.

Dining chairs: 'Saki', £79 plus £13 for natural cushions from Heals, 196 Tottenham Court Road, London, W1 and branches.

China display cabinet: Door panels (and chimney breast opposite) painted in Dulux Matchmaker 1018, back mirror panel and glass shelves from Chiswick Lane Glass, 42–44 Chiswick Lane, London, W4. Tel: 01-994-5779. Moulding on doors and chimney breast, no. 117, £3ft from Thomas & Wilson, 454 Fulham Road, London, SW6. Tel: 01-381-1161. Track for sliding door from Pelling & Cross, 93–103 Drummond Street, London, NW1. Tel: 01-380-1144.

Lighting: Shetland 2-light brass fitting £245, Hallam table lamps £114.50 each, toggle light switch on wall £17.50 from Christopher Wray's 600 Kings Road, London, SW6 (and branches). Tel: 01-736-8434. Parchment-effect shades from Material Effects, 15 Bellevue Road, London, SW17. Tel: 01-767-2241.

Curtains: made in Mirage glazed cotton £10.50m by Material Effects from Sanderson (address as before.)

Rope trimming: from Distinctive Trimmings.

Brass tubing and fittings for picture display structures and fireplace rails: from Beardmore, 3–4 Percy Street, London, W1. Tel: 01-637-7041.

Brass plates: £7.95 each from Heals (address as before).

Mick Hurd

Decorative painting: room, china display cabinet and curtains by Mick Hurd who will undertake commissions for total paint treatment transformation of interiors. He used a mixture of vivid emulsion paints from J. W. Bollom: Inspiration, Poppy, Canary, Golden, Orient Regal, Ultraviolet. Mick Hurd. Tel: 01-226-5857. J. W. Bollom, 13 Theobolds Road, London, WC1. Tel: 01-242-0313.

Display cabinet: built to commission by Adrian Thatcher. Tel: 01-221-7337.

Curtains: cotton duck fabric £1.93m, from Russell & Chapple, 23 Monmouth Street, London, WC2.

Butter muslin: (for unpainted window draping) £0.86m from McCulloch & Wallace, 25–26 Dering Street, London, W1.

Grate and marble surround: from a selection (subject to availability) at LASSco (Architectural Salvage), Mark Street, London, EC2. Tel: 01-739-0448.

Enamel and gold chandelier: 19th century Bohemian, £12,000, from Avi Zacaim, 48 Islington High Street, London, N1.

Lustres (on table): £2,000 the pair. As above.

China display cabinet: MDF supplied by Aronsson Brothers, Aro House, 18–19 Long Lane, London, EC1. Tel: 01-606-8050. Wood from Texas Home Care, branches throughout the country. Moulding from Newsons Timber Merchants, 61 Pimlico Road, London, SW1. Tel: 01-730-6262.

Bedroom

Stephen Calloway

Paint: Crown Colour Cue Stripes, XP-P & C12P emulsion, from Crown Paints. Tel: 0254–74951.

Floor: Oak Safir Wasa by Tarkett, approx £25sq m Tel: 0753-684533.

Bed: 'Patrice' by Vi-Spring. Tel: 0742-366311.

Pillows: Slumberdown. Tel: 0506-855899.

Metal spine chairs: designed by André Dubreuil, £575 each, from Themes & Variations, 231 Westbourne Grove, London, W11. Tel: 01-727-5531.

Firegrate & brass fender: Amazing Grates, 61 High Road, London, N2. Tel: 01-883-9590.

Mirror panels: Chelsea Glass, 66 Portslade Road, London, SW8.

Window drapes, baldechinos, bed, dressing table, mantelpiece & picture draperies: Material Effects, 15 Bellevue Road, London SW17. Tel: 01-767-2241.

Fabrics: Grey cotton sateen from John Lewis, £3.25m Oxford Street, London, W1, and branches.

White spotted net, £4.50m, from Alexanders, 32 Wentworth Street, London, E1. Tel: 01-247-5176.

Tassel fringe in 'smoke' by Laura Ashley, 183 Sloane Street, London, SW1 and branches. Tel: 01-235-9728.

Brass rail over picture & brass ombras (tiebacks): Beardmores, 3–4 Percy Street, London, W1. Tel: 01-637-7041.

Brass doorknobs & bellpush: Knobs & Knockers. Tel: 01-278-8925.

Antique French glass drop chandelier: around £450 from Sylvia Napier Ltd., 32 Ledbury Street, London, W11. Tel: 01-229-9986.

White candlesticks: about £35 each from Woolpit Interiors, Woolpit, Bury St. Edmunds, IP30 9SA. Tel: 0359-40895.

Bedside candlestick lamps: £20 each from Jane Churchill, 137 Sloane Street, London, SW1. Tel: 01-824-8484.

Vase (with lilies): by Oriel Harwood to order from the South Bank Crafts Centre, 164–167 Hungerford Arches, Royal Festival Hall, London, SE1. Tel: 01-928-0681.

Plants in conservatory: by Clifton Nurseries, Clifton Villas, Warwick Avenue, London, W9. Tel: 01-289-6851.

Antiques (on dressing table): 1920s perfume bottle with silver-top and 3 glass jars with silver-plated lids from Virginia Antiques, 98 Portland Road, London, W11. Tel: 01-727-9908.

3 cut glass perfume bottles with silver lids from Goldsmith and Perris, Stand 327, Alfies Antique Market, Marylebone, London, NW8. Tel: 01-724-7051.

Silver handmirror, silver-plated photoframe, plain glass bottles with silver lids and silver-backed hairbrush from Hythe Antique Centre, 5 High Street, Hythe, Kent. Tel: 0303-69643.

Cressida Bell

Paint: Crown Colour Cue, K1-11P & X2-1P emulsions, from Crown Paints. Tel: 0254-74951.

Carpet: Sanderson Super Hostess in Cornflower £18.75m from 52 Berners Street, London, W1. Tel: 01-535-7800.

Bed: 'Patrice' by Vi-Spring. Tel: 0742-366311.

Duvet & pillows: Slumberdown. Tel: 0506-855899.

Grate: Amazing Grates, 61 High Road, London, N2. Tel: 01-883-9590.

Snowdon armchair: covered in Smoke Dobby fabric, £445, from Laura Ashley, 183 Sloane Street, London, SW1 and branches. Tel: 01-235-9728.

Bedside table: This n' That, 50–51 Chalk Farm Road, London, NW1. Tel: 01-267-5433.

Dressing table: from This n' That (address as before) painted by C. Bell, 32 Fortescue Avenue, London, E8. Tel: 01-985-5863.

Hand-printed fabric for curtains, bedspread, tablecloth & cushions: designed by Cressida Bell and available to order for around £20m from Cressida Bell Ltd (address as before).

Curtain track: Swish.

Blinds: 'Filtashade' made to measure by Swish. *Curtain tiebacks:* Laura Ashley (address as before).

Standard lampbase: £31 from John Lewis, Oxford Street, London, W1 and branches.

Bedside lampbase: £12.95, from Laura Ashley (address as before).

Shades: Cressida Bell Ltd (address as before).

Overmantel mirror, lg. grey vase, shells, mantelpiece ornaments & silk flowers: Graham & Green, 4 Elgin Crescent, London, W11. Tel: 01-727-4594.

Miscellaneous: Antique cream silk shawl and fox fur draped over dummy; wooden painted rose dish on dressing table, papier-maché pen tray, 4 blue wooden egg cups, round tin on dressing table, blue ostrich feather & jug at bedside, blue chiffon handkerchief on dress. T. framed photo on mantelpiece all from Diana Maskell, Art & Antiques, High Street, Wadhurst, Kent. Tel: Wadhurst 2091.

Talc, soaps, pot pourri, cologne for men, powder puff & bath gel (on dressing table): Heals, 196 Tottenham Court Road, London, W1.

Nicholas Haslam

Paint: Sanderson Spectrum; walls 4–15M & 4-14P, panel mouldings & shutters 25–18D, from 52 Berners Street, London, W1. Tel: 01–636-7800.

Carpet: – Super Duchess 2230 in Stone Beige, approx. £18.50sq m from Victoria Carpets. Tel: 0562-823400.

Bed: 'Patrice' by Vi-Spring. Tel: 0742-366311.

Pillows: Slumberdown. Tel: 0506-855899.

Shutters: Plantation.

Curtains (on window): made in Longford Mid-Blue fabric, £26.50m from Colefax & Fowler, 39 Brook Street, London, W1 and branches. Tel: 01-493-2231.

Curtains over bed made by Colefax & Fowler in Bibury fabric, £13.50m see above; and by Warners in Middlehurst, £18.25m, 7–11 Noel Street, London, W1. Tel: 01-439-7012.

Net Curtains: from John Lewis, in beige Rhone, £4.95m, made by Swags, Studio 23, Abbey Business Centre, 15–17 Ingate Place, London, SW8. Tel: 01-720-2183.

Tudor wooden curtain poles: Harrison Drape.

Daybed: covered in Middlehurst, by Warners, about £670, made by Clements Interiors, 63 Queenstown Road, London, SW9. Tel: 01-627-4336.

Bookcase: £850 from Joanna Wood, 48 Pimlico Road, London, SW1. Tel: 01-486-3150.

French (upright) chairs: approx £280 each, from Ilexhurst, covered Warners Middlehurst, £18.25m, Unit 2, Glenville Mews, Kimber Road, London, SW18. Tel: 01-879-9830.

Headboard: approx £310 from Ilexhurst covered in Longford mid-blue by Colefax & Fowler (address as before).

Fireside chair: approx £330 from Ilexhurst in Longford mid-blue, Colefax & Fowler (address as before).

Bench: approx. £250, from Ilexhurst, covered Warners Middlehurst, £18.25m, (address as before).

Bedside tables: approx. £300 each from Ilexhurst (address as before).

Lamps: floor standing Viceroy lamp with green shade £90 and Somerville lamp with black shade, £39, from Christopher Wray, 600 Kings Road, London, SW6. Tel: 01-736-8434.

Overmantel Stratford mirror: £67 from John Lewis, Oxford Street, London, W1 and branches.

Black and gold Tenshu lampbase (on table): £29 and shade about £10, from John Lewis (address as above).

Bedside blue and white Prunus lampbases: £17.50 each, from John Lewis. Shade made by Lion, Witch & Lampshade covered in Primrose Mikado fabric, £4.45m, from John Lewis (address as above).

Tablecloth & cushion cover: in Aruba Damask in French Blue by Warners £15.95m made by Swags (address as before).

Lace & cotton bedlinen, lace cushion & wool bedcover from The Sleeping Company, 65 Wigmore Street, London, W1. Tel: 01-486-3150.

Yellow cushions: covered in Mikado fabric in Primrose, £4.45 m, from John Lewis (address as above).

Botanical flower prints: £35 each, from Jane Churchill, 137 Sloane Street, London, SW1. Tel: 01-824-8484.

Staffordshire dogs (on mantelpiece): £17.50 each from General Trading Company (GTC), 144 Sloane Street, London, SW1. Tel: 01-730-0411.

Miscellaneous: 1 large round silver frame, 2 papier-maché trinket boxes, oriental bowl with pot pourri from General Trading Company (address as above).

Miscellaneous (all on or around mantelpiece): Plate, black trinket pot with silver initial on top, small posy vase in white china, 2 black framed photos, 1 miniature photograph in case, 2 small frames at side of fireplace from Hythe Antique Centre, 5 High Street, Hythe, Kent. Tel: 0303-69643.

Tobacco jar (on bedside table): Hythe Antique Centre (address as above).

Oval silver frame: from General Trading Company (address as above).

Flat burgundy leather jewellery case, leather bound books, miniature photo in case, vase: Hythe Antique Centre (address as above).

Old enamelled tin, 2 leather bound books (on bookshelves): Hythe Antique Centre (address as above).

Leather bound books (on laundry basket): from Hythe Antique Centre (address as above).

3 blue & white plates (on corner shelves): from Hythe Antique Centre (address as above).

Victorian candlestick & blue/white trinket pot, vase: from Hythe Antique Centre (address as above).

Small oblong silver frame: from Goldsmith & Perris at Alfies Antique Market, Marylebone, NW8. Tel: 01-724-7951.

Large silver oblong frame (on round table): from Goldsmith & Perris at Alfies Antique Market (address as above).

Child's Room

Annie Sloan

Paint: base Dulux white emulsion. Cloud effect achieved with car spray paint. Tel: 0753-31151.

Cord carpet: 'Kaleidoscope' in Electric Blue, £3.25sq m, from Allied Carpets. Branches throughout the U.K.

Furniture: Connections range; Bunkbeds with L-shape conversion kit approx £280, desk approx £135, under bunk shelf with strip light approx £47, desk top approx £43, bookshelf (on end of bunk) approx £29, under bed storage boxes approx £31 each, stool approx £62, by Heartwood Furniture, Stretton Way, Wilson Road, Huyton, Liverpool, L36 6IX. Tel: 051-480-4929.

Duvet cover and pillowcase (upper bunk): plain blue, from John Lewis, Oxford Street, London, W1 and branches.

Pillows and duvets from Slumberdown. Tel: 0506-855899.

Matching duvet covers and pillowcases: £21.50 and £3.95 respectively, from Hippo Hall, The Peeking Hippo, 47 Palliser Road, London, W14. Tel: 01-381-4837.

Curtains: made by Swags in Aeroplanes cotton £7.50m from Hippo Hall (address as above).

Wooden blocks, books, blue cat toy car, Pooh Bear bookends, pull-along trains: from the General Trading Company, 144 Sloane Street, London, SW1. Tel: 01-730-0411.

Toys: hexagon card drum box with soldiers, Escor horse and rider, paint, palette and brushes, chalks, brio wooden train set, red plastic truck, aeroplane mobile, brown Steiff teddy, Kiddicraft action tractor: from Tridias, 6 Lichfield Terrace, Sheen Road, Richmond, Surrey and branches. Tel: 01-948-3459.

Jon Lys Turner

Paint effect: Dulux Matchmakers stainwood nos. 1428, 1187, 1345, 1054, 1570, 1166, 1170 and scumble glaze from J. W. Bollom, 13 Theobalds Road, London, WC1. Tel: 01-242-0313.

Oak flooring: in 'Nordic White', approx £25sq m, by Tarkett. Tel: 0753-684533.

Rug: by Jon Lys Turner, from Kingcome, 13 Walton Street, London, SW3. Tel: 01-589-8414.

Bed: by Vi-Spring. Tel: 0752-366311.

Duvet and pillows: by Slumberland. Tel: 0506-855899.

Duvet cover and pillowcase: by Jon Lys Turner, from Liberty's, Regent Street, London, W1 and branches. Tel: 01-734-1234.

Round table: £425, from Freud, 198 Shaftesbury Avenue, London, W1. Tel: 01-831-1071.

High-backed chairs: £250 each from Freud (address as above).

White Venetian blinds: made to measure from Sunstor. Tel: 0705-750212

Black lamp: £59.95, from Lightstyle, 94 Tottenham Court Road, London, W1. Tel: 01-637-4858.

Wall lights: made by Jon Lys Turner from terracotta planters, approx. £6 from Patio, 155 Battersea Park Road, London, SW8.

Mosaic wall transfers: 6in × 6in, in drawers by Jon Lys Turner blown up on a photocopier.

Antique toy collection: loaned by Michael Duarden.

Antique medicine cabinet: designer's own.

Toys and pinboard: from Habitat, 196 Tottenham Court Road, London W1 and branches throughout the U.K.

Postcards: from Victoria & Albert Museum shop, Exhibition Road, London, SW8.

Floella Benjamin

Paint: Dulux Matchmakers no. 1154 and 1489 and Poppy gloss. Tel: 0753-31151.

Wallpaper: American Country Kids no. 96251, £18.34 per roll, from Paper Moon, 53 Fairfax Road, London, NW6. Tel: 01-634-1198.

Vinyl floor tiles: in red and yellow, £7.75 per pack of 9, from Habitat, 196 Tottenham Court Road, London, W1 and branches.

Green sofabed: (converts to 2 single or double bed) from Connection range, approx £399, by Heartwood Furniture, Stretton Way, Wilson Road, Huyton, Liverpool, L36 6JX. Tel: 051-480-4929.

Duvet and pillow: from Slumberdown. Tel: 0506-855899.

Miscellaneous: sheet: £10.99; pillowcase: £3.99; duvet cover: £26.99; moon, knot and pyramid cushions: £2.99 each; rugs: £4.99 each; green curtains: £16.99 pair; clock: £14.99; lamp: £7.99; yellow mini-bin: £2.99; cost peg rack: £3.99; felt animal wall decorations and plastic storage boxes: all from the Krazy Kombination range at Kidstore, 327/329 Harrow Road, London, W9 (and branches). Items subject to availability due to seasonal changes in ranges.

Wardrobe: £159, *blanket box:* £99 and *pini blind:* £14.95 from Habitat (address as above).

Spur shelving brackets and plywood for shelving: from B&Q DIY branches throughout the U.K.

Seashore mural: used Dulux Matchmaker emulsions, made by J. B. Designs (wide variety of commissions undertaken including murals and tile painting), Hide Barn, The Hale, Wendover, Bucks. Tel: 0296-625419.

Clothes and shoes: from Mothercare. Branches throughout the U.K.

Toys: from Tridias, 6 Lichfield Terrace, Sheen Road, Richmond, Surrey and branches. Tel: 01-948-3459.

Bathroom

Doug Patterson

Tiles: from the floor up: Hereford Royal Blue
£23.37sq m, Empire Blue Diamond £25sq m,
Empire Blue Squares £25sq m, Dimpled bright
white £13.48sq m, Hereford Satin Blue
£16.17sq m, from Worlds End Tiles, 9 Langton
Street, London, SW10. Tel: 01-351-0279.

Mosaic tiles: ref. KA 32 £17.84sq m. As previous.

Victoria border tiles: £1 each approx, from
Dennis Ruabon Ltd. Tel: 0978-843484.

Vinyl flooring: from Tarkett. Tel: 0753-684533.

Lido bath: £750, *Tulip WC:* £160, *Marmara (shell)
handbasin:* £100, *Corner basin (grotto):* £70,
*Monoblock basin mixer, Monolux bath/shower
mixer:* all from Ideal Standard (all prices approx)
Tel: 0482-46461.

Miscellaneous: extending mirrors: £45 each,
18" long glass & chrome shelves: £11.70 each,
24" towel rails: £8.50 each, pearl shell soap dish
(in grotto): £6.95, pedal bin: £7.50, shower
curtains: 'Jonelle' £15 each, Austrian blind: ready
made in seersucker £65, white towels: all from
John Lewis, Oxford Street, London, W1 and
branches.

Mirror panel: from Capital Glazing, 357 Old
Kent Road, London, SE1. Tel: 01-237-1219.

Rococo shell wall lights: £52.13 each, from Last
Detail. 341 Kings Road, London, SW3.

Low voltage halogen mini-spots (illuminating
grotto): from Concord Lighting, 241 City Road,
London, EC1.

Pewter candelabras: £53.95, from the Pewter
Shop, 16 Burlington Arcade, London, W1.
Tel: 01-493-1730.

Black candles from Heals, 196 Tottenham Court
Road, London, W1 and branches.

Grotesque wall fountain: £36 plus delivery,
direct from Haddonstone, The Forge House,
Church Lane, East Haddon, Northampton,
NN6 8DB. Tel: 0604-770365.

Towels, bathrobe and silver-grey tiebacks: from
John Lewis (address as above).

Shell stencils on floor: cut & painted by Anne
Glaskin & Eddie Anderson of Pavilion. 2-part
small shell stencil (8" × 8") designed for the

programme is available as a special offer from
Pavilion for £6.75 inc. postage. Catalogue of over
50 ready cut designs available for £1.00. 6a Howe
Street, Edinburgh. Tel: 031-225-3590. Also
available from Paperchase, Tottenham Court
Road, London, W1.

Shells on grotto arch: £0.30 – £1.00 each, from
Eaton's Shell Shops 16 Manette Street, London,
W1.

Ferns: From Clifton Nurseries, Clifton Villas,
Warwick Ave, London, W9. Tel: 01-289-6851.

Miscellaneous: natural sponges, loofah, pewter
shaving mug, brush & razor, selection of
aftershaves & colognes, hair conditioners &
soaps from selection at George F. Trumper,
9 Curzon Street, London, W1. Tel: 01-499-1850.

Althea Wilson

Sponged wall finish: by Althea Wilson (using
own mix of paint).

White tiles: painted and glazed with 'On Glaze'
by Althea Wilson, supplied by Johnson & Johnson
Ltd, Stoke on Trent. Tel: 0782-575575.

Floor: 'Pave', Balanor vinyl, £5.75 approx sq m,
from Sommer Allibert, Berry Hill Industrial
Estate, Droitwich, Worcs, WR9 9AB.
Tel: 0905-774221.

Steel bath: Ariston, £55. Tel: 0494-459711.

W.C. and handbasin: Fiesta WC, £70; basin, £38
from Trent Bathrooms. Tel: 0782-202123.

Bath/shower mixer and basin taps: mixer £55,
taps £17 from Tantafex. Tel: 0342-28166.

Chrome picture light: £68.95 from Mr Light,
275 Fulham Road, London, SW10.

White roller blind: painted by AW, by Sunstor.
Tel: 0705-750212.

Miscellaneous: towels, bathmat, flannels,
bathrobe, toothpaste, mug soap dish, soaps, bath
oils, creams: from John Lewis, Oxford Street,
London W1 and branches.

Glass vase: from Habitat, 196 Tottenham Court
Road, London, W1 and branches.

Blue dried flowers: from John Lewis (address as
above).

Old chemist's bottle with glass stopper: filled
with blue bubble bath, Hythe Antiques Centre,
5 High Street, Hythe, Kent. Tel: 0303-69643.

Mary Fox Linton

White paint: from Dulux. Tel: 0753-31151.

Wallpaper: Osaka 8057 £14.95 a roll, by Today
Interiors, 146 New Cavendish Street, London,
W1. Tel: 01-636-0541.

White tiles: painted by Althea Wilson,
from Johnson & Johnson. Tel: 0782 575575.

Carpet: Super Suede Lamsfleece, approx.
£21.95sq m, by Victoria Carpets. Tel:
0562-823400.

Pressed steel bath: approx. £100, from
C. P. Hart, Newnham Terrace, Hercules Road,
London, SE1. Tel: 01-928-5866.

Bath/shower mixer: £149.80, *Basin Taps:* £71.80
and *Tulip WC:* £160, (all prices approx) from
Ideal Standard. Tel: 0482-46461.

Shower curtains: 'Jonelle', £15 each, from John
Lewis, Oxford Street, London, W1 and
branches.

*Vanity unit with drawers cupboard and inset
sink:* £450 approx, by Franke Bathrooms from
Eurospa, 32–33 Victoria Road, Surbiton, Surrey.
Tel: 01-390-1377.

Perspex knobs: by Knobs & Knockers. Tel:
01-278-8925.

White microblinds: (window & sides of bath) by
Luxaflex. Tel: 0932-228822.

Mirrors and glass shelves: by Chelsea Glass,
650 Portslade Road, London, SW8. Tel:
01-581-2501.

Ceramic and chrome soap dish: £29.50, from the
Conran Shop, Michelin House, 81 Fulham Road,
London, SW3.

White towels, flannels and bathmat: from Next.
Branches around the UK.

White alabaster jars & dishes (on shelves above
end of bath): from Mary Fox Linton Assoc,
249 Fulham Road, London, SW3.

Stainless steel toothbrush mug: one of set of 4 in
leather case, from Heals, 196 Tottenham Court
Road, London, W1 and branches.

Shaving brush and mug: from Heals (address as
above).

Index

Acknowledgements

The Publishers would like to thank Alex Corrin for indexing, Anne-Marie and the boys at Graham Henderson Photography for their help, Geoff Dan and Susanna Price for additional photography, and Carole Pegg for all her hard work.

The Thames Television programme ROOM FOR CHANGE was presented by Peter Leonard of Soho Designs.

The Thames Television Production Team: Anne Clements, David Bellamy, Fiona McCrae, Renny Harrop and Rose Ashfield.